LEAD, KINDLY LIGHT

THE
NOTRE
DAME
BOOK
OF
PRAYERS

EDITED BY JOHN AND SYLVIA DILLON

CAMPUS MINISTRY, UNIVERSITY OF NOTRE DAME

Lead, kindly Light, amid the encircling gloom,
Lead Thou me on!
The night is dark, and I am far from home—
Lead Thou me on!
Keep Thou my feet; I do not ask to see
The distant scene—one step enough for me.

I was not ever thus, nor prayed that Thou
Shouldst lead me on.
I loved to choose and see my path; but now,
Lead Thou me on!
I loved the garish day, and, spite of fears,
Pride ruled my will: remember not past years.

So long Thy power hath blessed me, sure it still
Will lead me on,
O'er moor and fen, o'er crag and torrent, till
The night is gone;
And with the morn those angel faces smile
Which I have loved long since, and lost awhile.

Published 1871
JOHN HENRY CARDINAL NEWMAN
(1801-1890)

Contents

Dedication

It is with deep love and respect that we dedicate this Notre Dame book of prayers, *Lead, Kindly Light*, to **Rev. Richard V. Warner, c.s.c.** Having served as director of Campus Ministry for the past 15 years, Father Warner has worked tirelessly to build a vibrant ministerial presence to serve the personal and spiritual needs of students, staff, and alumni. His visionary leadership and passionate commitment to evangelization infuse all of Campus Ministry's efforts and are testament to both his profound faith and sincere love of the Church. It is through his guidance and support that this prayer book is made available to every student who enters the University.

The fact that Father Warner would never seek praise or thanks for his good work makes this dedication all the more significant for those of us who have the privilege of working with him.

General Introduction

What you hold in your hands is the 2005 Notre Dame book of prayers, edited through Campus Ministry. Many of the selections are original prayers written by current

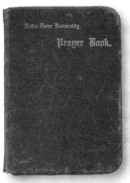

1899

and past members of the Notre Dame family—students, faculty members, administrators, employees, and alumni. Notre Dame prayer books date back to 1899, and while each is somewhat different in style and composition, all are part of an ongoing tradition that seeks to provide students with a guide to prayer and an opportunity to deepen their spiritual lives. A Notre Dame alumnus once wrote about keeping a copy of the 1942 prayer book in the lining of his helmet as a source of comfort and strength during World War II.

This newest prayer book, *Lead, Kindly Light,* is designed to encourage a habit of daily prayer, focusing on the moments and seasons celebrated here at Notre Dame and in the larger church community, as well as on the issues and concerns that seem central to the many people who responded to our efforts to collect prayers. Its artwork and images are also a call to prayer. The campus is filled with images that remind us of God's presence—both in natural beauty and in artwork. A key to the images used throughout can be found at the back of the book.

Prayer is one of our most powerful connections with God and the way that we both celebrate the good and struggle against the evil, within and without, that is the reality of our lives. We hope that prayer will be a central part of your experience while here at Notre Dame and in all your future experiences. May this prayer book become well-worn, dog-eared, and written in, a treasured keepsake of your time spent here at Notre Dame, and a constant guide and source of inspiration and comfort for years to come.

1942

Praying to Begin and End the Day

As in any good relationship of friends or lovers, frequent communication nurtures and strengthens that bond. So it is in our relationship with God. We desire to speak to God, to listen for God's words in our lives and ultimately to know God's will for us.

This section of the prayer book is designed to foster a daily routine of prayer in the morning and at night—perhaps 10 quiet minutes to begin and end each day in God's presence.

A central theme shapes the prayer for each day with original prayers, psalms, and scripture to guide your meditation. Follow the days of the week in order, or let your heart lead you to the theme that best meets your needs.

SUNDAY MORNING

RESURRECTION

This is the day the Lord has made;
Let us rejoice and be glad.

SIMPLE DAILY PRAYER

Lord,
Help us to see in each other
and be for each other
the unending light of Christ. Amen

KATE ROWLAND KOZMINSKI, *2000 alumna*

2 CORINTHIANS 4:6-11

Brothers and sisters:
God who said, *Let light shine out of darkness,*
has shone in our hearts to bring to light
the knowledge of the glory of God
on the face of Jesus Christ.
But we hold this treasure in earthen vessels,
that the surpassing power may be of God
and not from us.
We are afflicted in every way, but not constrained;
perplexed, but not driven to despair;
persecuted, but not abandoned;

struck down, but not destroyed;
  always carrying about in the body
    the dying of Jesus, so that the life of Jesus
may also be manifested in our body.
For we who live are constantly being given up to death
    for the sake of Jesus,
  so that the life of Jesus may be manifested
    in our mortal flesh.

ANTIPHON

All the ends of the earth
have seen the salvation by our God.

PSALM 98:1,2-4

Sing to the LORD a new song,
  for he has done wondrous deeds;
his right hand has won victory for him,
  his holy arm.
The LORD has made his salvation known:
  in the sight of the nations he has revealed his justice.
He has remembered his kindness and his faithfulness
  toward the house of Israel.
All the ends of the earth have seen
  the salvation by our God.
Sing joyfully to the LORD, all you lands;
  break into song; sing praise.

GLORY TO THE FATHER, and to the Son,
    and to the Holy Spirit,
as it was in the beginning, is now,
    and will be for ever. Amen.

CLOSING PRAYER

God of mercy,
by the outpouring of your love
    you give us new birth in the Spirit,
    and redeem us in the blood of Christ.
Increase our awareness of these blessings,
    and renew your gift of life within us.
We ask these things in the name of Jesus Christ,
    our Lord and Redeemer. Amen.

*Prayer is an expression of who we are.
    We are a living incompleteness.
We are a gap, an emptiness
that calls for fulfillment.*

THOMAS MERTON

SUNDAY EVENING

RESURRECTION

This is the day the Lord has made;
Let us rejoice and be glad.

LOVE, HOPE, AND PEACE

Lord,
Please grant me the grace to be
    a witness of your love,
        a sign of your hope,
    and the presence of your peace. Amen.

WALTER PRUCHNIK, *O'Neill Family Hall*

1 PETER 1:3-9

Blessed be the God and Father of our Lord Jesus Christ,
    who in his great mercy gave us a new birth
        to a living hope
through the resurrection of Jesus Christ from the dead,
    to an inheritance that is imperishable,
        undefiled, and unfading,
kept in heaven for you who by the power of God
    are safeguarded through faith,
to a salvation that is ready to be revealed
    in the final time.

In this you rejoice, although now for a little while
    you may have to suffer through various trials,
        so that the genuineness of your faith,
    more precious than gold that is perishable
        even though tested by fire,
    may prove to be for praise, glory, and honor
        at the revelation of Jesus Christ.
Although you have not seen him you love him;
    even though you do not see him now
        yet believe in him,
    you rejoice with an indescribable and glorious joy,
    as you attain the goal of your faith,
        the salvation of your souls.

ANTIPHON

Say to the Lord, "My refuge and my fortress; my God,
in whom I trust."

PSALM 91:1-2,10-15

You who live in the shelter of the Most High,
    who abide in the shadow of the Almighty,
will say to the Lord, "My refuge and my fortress;
    my God, in whom I trust."
No evil shall befall you,
    no scourge come near your tent.
For he will command his angels concerning you
    to guard you in all your ways.
On their hands they will bear you up,
    so that you will not dash your foot against a stone.

You will tread on the lion and the adder,
    the young lion and the serpent
        you will trample under foot.
Those who love me, I will deliver;
    I will protect those who know my name.
When they call to me, I will answer them;
    I will be with them in trouble,
        I will rescue them and honor them.

GLORY TO THE FATHER, and to the Son,
    and to the Holy Spirit,
as it was in the beginning, is now,
    and will be for ever. Amen.

CLOSING PRAYER

Almighty and Eternal God,
    through the power of your goodness
        we have been saved from death and given new life.
Look on us with mercy and favor
    and bring lasting salvation to all humankind.
Let the world see that, in you,
    the broken are made whole
        and the fallen are lifted up.
May our celebration of Christ's victory
    over sin and death
        show its effects in the way we live our lives.
We ask these things in the name
    of our Redeemer and Lord, Jesus Christ. Amen.

*S*ome will find time for
  prayer in the evening.
At nightfall we have
  the day behind
and the night before us.
Prayer at that time is different
  from prayer in the morning
  as sentiments at sunset
  differ from those at sunrise.
There is no need to praise
  one time over the other.
The heart knows a time
  for both.

MARTIN HELLDORFER

MONDAY MORNING

PRAISE AND THANKSGIVING

Lord, open my lips,
and my mouth will proclaim your praise.

GOOD MORNING, LORD!

Good morning, Lord!
Thank you for this beautiful day.
I am blessed to have it to live to the fullest.
Help me to remember all those who love me
and to be grateful for your many gifts.
Let me please you in all that I do today, Lord.
Let me treat everyone fairly and equally.
Help me to have a positive attitude in everything I do,
and to persevere through tests, quizzes,
and all obstacles that I may encounter.
Be with me every step of the way,
guiding me to make wise decisions.
If I fail, forgive me, and help me to learn
from my mistakes.
I love you and thank you always. Amen.

STEPHANIE ANNE SMITH, *Walsh Hall*

PHILIPPIANS 4:4-7

Brothers and sisters:
Rejoice in the Lord always.
    I shall say it again: rejoice!
Your kindness should be known to all.
    The Lord is near.
Have no anxiety at all, but in everything,
    by prayer and petition, with thanksgiving,
    make your requests known to God.
Then the peace of God that surpasses all understanding
    will guard your hearts and your minds
    in Christ Jesus.

ANTIPHON

Awake, O my soul; awake, lyre and harp!
    I will wake the dawn.

PSALM 57:8-9,10,12

My heart is steadfast, O God;
my heart is steadfast;
    I will sing and chant praise.
Awake, O my soul; awake, lyre and harp!
    I will wake the dawn.
I will give thanks to you among the peoples, O LORD,
    I will chant your praise among the nations.

For your mercy towers to the heavens,
    and your faithfulness to the skies.
Be exalted above the heavens, O God;
    above all the earth be your glory!

GLORY TO THE FATHER, and to the Son,
    and to the Holy Spirit,
as it was in the beginning, is now,
    and will be for ever. Amen.

CLOSING PRAYER

God, my friend,
I offer you this day.
Let all my prayer, work, joy, and suffering today
    join with the lives offered to you
        by the whole People of God
    and especially with your great Eucharist,
        Jesus, your Son and our brother.
Let your Spirit be with me today,
    especially in….
And I ask your loving concern today,
    especially for….
Remind me, through the day, that I am not alone.
Grant this through Christ, our Lord. Amen.

REV. WILLIAM J. O'MALLEY, S.J.

MONDAY EVENING

PRAISE AND THANKSGIVING

Lord, open my lips,
and my mouth will proclaim your praise.

IN THANKSGIVING

Loving God,
    oftentimes I take so much for granted.
I turn to you in times of sorrow
    and forget to turn to you in times of joy as well.
I thank you for my life,
    for I can be your tabernacle and apostle
        spreading joy, peace, and love.
I thank you for my family and friends,
    for they are towers of support.
I thank you for this day,
        because it was filled with opportunity
    to use my gifts in your service
        and according to your will.
Lord, I am grateful for the miracles
    that I witness every day—
        from the setting sun to the kindness of a stranger.
Please give me the eyes to see
    and the humility to voice my thanks
        in the best way I know how. Amen.

ARINA GROSSU, *McGlinn Hall*

COLOSSIANS 3: 15-17

And let the peace of Christ control your hearts,
 the peace into which you were also called in one body.
And be thankful.
Let the word of Christ dwell in you richly,
 as in all wisdom you teach and admonish one another,
  singing psalms, hymns, and spiritual songs
 with gratitude in your hearts to God.
And whatever you do, in word or in deed,
 do everything in the name of the Lord Jesus,
  giving thanks to God the Father through him.

ANTIPHON

In the shadow of your wings I shout for joy.

PSALM 63: 5-8

Thus I will bless you while I live;
 lifting up my hands, I will call upon your name.
As with the riches of a banquet shall my soul be satisfied,
 and with exultant lips my mouth shall praise you.
I will remember you upon my couch,
 and through the night-watches I will meditate on you:
you are my help,
 and in the shadow of your wings I shout for joy.

GLORY TO THE FATHER, and to the Son,
    and to the Holy Spirit,
as it was in the beginning, is now,
    and will be for ever. Amen.

CLOSING PRAYER

For all your creatures, in all your creatures,
    we praise you.
We give you thanks for the sun, the moon, and the stars,
    for the air we breathe and the land that nourishes us.
And most of all, in each other,
    for each other, we thank and praise you,
        the Lord of Creation. Amen.

ST. FRANCIS OF ASSISI

For me, prayer is a surge of the heart;
* it is a simple look toward heaven,*
it is a cry of recognition and of love,
embracing both trial and joy.

ST. THERESE OF LISIEUX

TUESDAY MORNING

DISCIPLESHIP

Lord, let the light of your glory shine within us,
and lead us to the joy of life in you.

THE DAY AWAITS

As I open my eyes from sleep,
    help me to see you in everyone and
    everything I encounter today.
I stand before this day
    unaware of your will for me.
Lead me to opportunities where I can embrace
    the challenge to serve you.
Give me the strength to accept those opportunities
    with a loving heart and an outstretched hand.
Be with me, through the obstacles, frustrations,
    and rewards that this day will hold.
And give me the wisdom to find peace,
    even amidst chaos.
May the morning air bring life to my body
    and joy to my soul.
Amen.

JENNY TILGHMAN, *1995 Alumna*

MATTHEW 10:26–33

Jesus said to the Twelve:
    "Fear no one.
Nothing is concealed that will not be revealed,
    nor secret that will not be known.
What I say to you in the darkness, speak in the light;
    what you hear whispered, proclaim on the housetops.
And do not be afraid of those who kill the body but
    cannot kill the soul;
        rather, be afraid of the one who can destroy
    both soul and body in Gehenna.
Are not two sparrows sold for a small coin?
Yet not one of them falls to the ground
    without your Father's knowledge.
Even all the hairs of your head are counted.
So do not be afraid; you are worth more than
    many sparrows.
Everyone who acknowledges me before others
    I will acknowledge before my heavenly Father.
But whoever denies me before others,
    I will deny before my heavenly Father."

ANTIPHON

The mouths of the righteous utter wisdom.

PSALM 37:3–6, 30–31

Trust in the Lord, and do good;
    so you will live in the land and enjoy security.

Take delight in the Lord,
  and he will give you the desires of your heart.
Commit your way to the Lord;
  trust in him, and he will act.
He will make your vindication shine like the light,
  and the justice of your cause like the noonday.
The mouths of the righteous utter wisdom,
  and their tongues speak justice.
The law of their God is in their hearts;
  their steps do not slip.

GLORY TO THE FATHER, and to the Son,
  and to the Holy Spirit,
as it was in the beginning, is now,
  and will be for ever. Amen.

CLOSING PRAYER

We bless you, Creator of all things,
  for you have given us the goods of the earth
    and brought us to this day.
Look with favor on us as we begin our daily work,
  let us be fellow workers with you.
Make our work today benefit our brothers and sisters,
  that with them and for them we may build
    an earthly city, pleasing to you.
Grant joy and peace to us,
  and to all we meet this day.
We ask this through Christ, our Lord. Amen.

CHRISTIAN PRAYER: THE LITURGY OF THE HOURS

TUESDAY EVENING

DISCIPLESHIP

*Lord, let the light of your glory shine within us,
    and lead us to the joy of life in you.*

SPIRIT

Spirit of Life,
permeate my body,
making me come alive
to bear witness to your
teachings by my actions.

Spirit of Love,
permeate my heart,
making me aware of your genuine love
poured out to me that I might
share this love with others.

Spirit of Hope,
permeate my soul,
guiding me in all my endeavors
to strive always to do
your will. Amen.

MARISSA MATTHEWS, *Cavanaugh Hall*

ROMANS 12:9-18

Brothers and sisters:
Let love be sincere;
    hate what is evil,
    hold on to what is good;
    love one another with mutual affection;
    anticipate one another in showing honor.
Do not grow slack in zeal,
    be fervent in spirit,
    serve the Lord.
Rejoice in hope,
    endure in affliction,
    persevere in prayer.
Contribute to the needs of the holy ones,
    exercise hospitality.
Bless those who persecute [you],
    bless and do not curse them.
Rejoice with those who rejoice,
  weep with those who weep.
Have the same regard for one another;
    do not be haughty but associate with the lowly;
    do not be wise in your own estimation.
Do not repay anyone evil for evil;
    be concerned for what is noble in the sight of all.
If possible, on your part, live at peace with all.

ANTIPHON

The law of the Lord is perfect, refreshing the soul.

PSALM 19:8-11

The law of the LORD is perfect,
    refreshing the soul;
the decree of the LORD is trustworthy,
    giving wisdom to the simple.
The precepts of the LORD are right,
    rejoicing the heart;
the command of the LORD is clear,
    enlightening the eye.
The fear of the LORD is pure,
    enduring forever;
the ordinances of the LORD are true,
    all of them just.
They are more precious than gold,
    than a heap of purest gold;
sweeter also than syrup
    or honey from the comb.

GLORY TO THE FATHER, and to the Son,
    and to the Holy Spirit,
as it was in the beginning, is now,
    and will be for ever. Amen.

CLOSING PRAYER

Be present, O merciful God,
    and protect us through the silent hours of this night,
so that we who are wearied
    by the changes and chances of this fleeting world
        may rest upon your eternal changelessness,
through Jesus Christ our Lord. Amen.

OXFORD BOOK OF PRAYER

*I*f, during prayer, you do nothing but bring your heart from distraction again and again into God's presence, though it went away every time you brought it back, your time would be very well spent.

ST. FRANCIS DE SALES

WEDNESDAY MORNING

DISCERNMENT

You have made us for yourself, O Lord,
and our hearts are restless until they rest in you.

PRAYER FOR DIRECTION

Lord,
We ask you to bless us with your gifts
of strength, patience, and faith.
Teach us to live with gratitude, joy, and love,
for each day is truly a blessing.
Inspire us to see your gift of life as a magnificent journey.
Help us to find peace and hope through the realization
that you are calling us,
guiding our talents to the needs of the world
through our own personal vocation.
Give us the confidence, O Lord, to trust in your will.
Amen.

KATIE REIJULA, *Off-Campus*

1 CORINTHIANS 1:26-31

Consider your own calling, brothers and sisters.
Not many of you were wise by human standards,
not many were powerful,
not many were of noble birth.

Rather, God chose the foolish of the world
   to shame the wise,
and God chose the weak of the world
   to shame the strong,
and God chose the lowly and despised of the world,
   those who count for nothing,
to reduce to nothing those who are something,
   so that no human being might boast before God.
It is due to him that you are in Christ Jesus,
   who became for us wisdom from God,
as well as righteousness, sanctification, and redemption,
   so that, as it is written,
"Whoever boasts, should boast in the Lord."

ANTIPHON

Guide me in your truth and teach me,
   for you are God my savior.

PSALM 25:4-5,8-9,10,14

Your ways, O LORD, make known to me;
   teach me your paths.
Guide me in your truth and teach me,
   for you are God my savior,
   and for you I wait all the day.
Good and upright is the LORD;
   thus he shows sinners the way.
He guides the humble to justice,
   and teaches the humble his way.

All the paths of the LORD are kindness and constancy
    toward those who keep his covenant and his decrees.
The friendship of the LORD is with those who fear him,
    and his covenant, for their instruction.

GLORY TO THE FATHER, and to the Son,
    and to the Holy Spirit,
as it was in the beginning, is now,
    and will be for ever. Amen.

CLOSING PRAYER

O gracious and holy Father,
give us the wisdom to perceive you,
intelligence to understand you,
diligence to seek you,
patience to wait for you,
eyes to see you,
a heart to meditate on you,
and a life to proclaim you,
through the power of the spirit of Jesus Christ our Lord.
Amen.

ST. BENEDICT

WEDNESDAY EVENING

DISCERNMENT

You have made us for yourself, O Lord,
and our hearts are restless until they rest in you.

YOUR GUIDING HAND

Lord,
I have felt your hand guiding me to this place.
Your love has strengthened me to face the challenges
    that lie ahead.
As I go into the world to serve you,
    may your spirit continue to lift me up.
When I feel alone, remind me that I am surrounded
    by a great cloud of witnesses
        who have set an example for me to follow.
When I lose my way, send your fire before me
    to guide me on my path.
When things go wrong, give me the courage
    to admit my mistakes and try again.
When I feel I cannot go on,
    show me that with your help I can do anything,
        for with your love and guidance I cannot fail.
In all things, at all times, may my life give glory to you.
    Amen.

REV. JONATHAN D. LAWRENCE, *Graduate Student*

DANIEL 2:20-23

Blessed be the name of God from age to age,
    for wisdom and power are his.
He changes times and seasons,
    deposes kings and sets up kings;
he gives wisdom to the wise
    and knowledge to those who have understanding.
He reveals deep and hidden things;
    he knows what is in the darkness,
    and light dwells with him.
To you, O God of my ancestors,
    I give thanks and praise....

from the NEW REVISED STANDARD VERSION

ANTIPHON

Probe me, God, and know my heart; try me,
    and know my thoughts.

PSALM 139:1B-3,13-14AB,23-24

O LORD, you have probed me, and you know me:
    you know when I sit and when I stand;
    you understand my thoughts from afar.
My journeys and my rest you scrutinize,
    with all my ways you are familiar.
Truly you have formed my inmost being;
    you knit me in my mother's womb.
I give you thanks that I am fearfully, wonderfully made;
    wonderful are your works.

Probe me, O God, and know my heart;
    try me, and know my thoughts;
See if my way is crooked,
    and lead me in the way of old.

GLORY TO THE FATHER, and to the Son,
    and to the Holy Spirit,
as it was in the beginning, is now,
    and will be for ever. Amen.

CLOSING PRAYER

Lord,
I am closing this day.
I am thinking of my failures and frustrations,
    deadlines and duties.
I feel like I have fallen behind, and I am tired.
You have called me to love you and to love others.
As I prepare to sleep, help me to see
    where I have served you today.
Help me to see where we met as I sped through my day.
Help me to find peace for a restful night
    in the knowledge that I have done some good today
        and that you are with me every moment. Amen.

DOMINIQUE SCHOTT BAROCO, *1997 Alumna*

THURSDAY MORNING

TRUST AND FAITH

Seek and you shall find,
knock and the door will be opened.

TRUST

Lord,
I often wonder how I'm going to make it through.
I worry about the little things,
and they all seem too difficult to handle.
Help me to remember, Lord,
that your Providence and Grace
are big enough for all my dreams and desires,
and then some.
Lord, help me to put my life truly in your hands
and to welcome the path you have traced for me.
Amen.

ANNE WATSON, *1999 Alumna*

MATTHEW 6:25-33

Jesus said to his disciples:
…"I tell you, do not worry about your life,
what you will eat or drink,
or about your body, what you will wear.

Is not life more than food and the body
    more than clothing?
Look at the birds in the sky;
    they do not sow or reap,
        they gather nothing into barns,
    yet your heavenly Father feeds them.
Are not you more important than they?
Can any of you by worrying add a single moment
    to your life-span?
Why are you anxious about clothes?
Learn from the way the wild flowers grow.
They do not work or spin.
But I tell you that not even Solomon in all his splendor
    was clothed like one of them.
If God so clothes the grass of the field,
    which grows today
        and is thrown into the oven tomorrow,
    will he not much more provide for you,
        O you of little faith?
So do not worry and say, 'What are we to eat?'
    or 'What are we to drink?' or 'What are we to wear?'
All these things the pagans seek.
Your heavenly Father knows that you need them all.
But seek first the kingdom of God and his righteousness,
    and all these things will be given you besides."

ANTIPHON

Wait for the Lord with courage; be stouthearted,
    and wait for the Lord.

PSALM 27:4,13-14

One thing I ask of the LORD; this I seek:
To dwell in the house of the LORD
    all the days of my life,
that I may gaze on the loveliness of the LORD
    and contemplate his temple.
I believe that I shall see the bounty of the LORD
    in the land of the living.
Wait for the LORD with courage;
    be stouthearted, and wait for the LORD.

GLORY TO THE FATHER, and to the Son,
    and to the Holy Spirit,
as it was in the beginning, is now,
    and will be for ever. Amen.

CLOSING PRAYER

May all I do today begin with you, O Lord.
Plant dreams and hopes within my soul,
    revive my tired spirit:
    be with me today.
May all I do today continue with your help, O Lord.
Be at my side and walk with me:
    be my support today.
May all I do today reach far and wide, O Lord.
My thoughts, my work, my life:
    make them blessings for your kingdom;
    let them go beyond today, O God. Amen.

PASSIONIST PUBLICATIONS

THURSDAY EVENING

TRUST AND FAITH

Seek and you shall find,
  knock and the door will be opened.

EVENING OFFERING

Lord,
please accept my simple prayer
  as I reach out to you for your loving grace.
Tonight I offer to you all my concerns and anxieties.
Please take them and turn them into joy.
Please let me know your loving kindness
  in the smallest of ways,
    a smile, a kind word, a song, a peaceful night.
Please let me be a sign of kindness
  to someone else in need.
I trust that you walk with me, right next to me, always.
Tomorrow, I know the dawn of a new day will bring
  brightness and hope. Amen.

MARIA SCHOTT HALLORAN, *1996 Alumna*

ROMANS 5:1-5

Brothers and sisters:
Therefore, since we have been justified by faith,
    we have peace with God through our Lord Jesus Christ,
through whom we have gained access by faith
    to this grace in which we stand,
        and we boast in hope of the glory of God.
Not only that, but we even boast of our afflictions,
    knowing that affliction produces endurance,
        and endurance, proven character,
    and proven character, hope,
        and hope does not disappoint,
because the love of God has been poured out into our hearts
        through the Holy Spirit that has been given to us.

ANTIPHON

Take courage and be stouthearted,
    all you who hope in the Lord.

PSALM 31:2-4,17,25

In you, O LORD, I take refuge;
    let me never be put to shame.
In your justice rescue me,
    incline your ear to me,
    make haste to deliver me!
Be my rock of refuge,
    a stronghold to give me safety.
You are my rock and my fortress;
    for your name's sake you will lead and guide me.

Let your face shine upon your servant;
     save me in your kindness.
Take courage and be stouthearted,
     all you who hope in the LORD.

GLORY TO THE FATHER, and to the Son,
     and to the Holy Spirit,
as it was in the beginning, is now,
     and will be for ever. Amen.

CLOSING PRAYER

O Lord,
you have been with me all through the day.
Now evening has come.
The shadows have lengthened into darkness.
Let my busy world grow quiet,
     the feverish concerns of my day be stilled,
          my work put away.
Kindest Lord Jesus,
grant me your grace
     that it may always be with me,
          and work with me, and stay with me to the end.
Grant that I may always desire and choose
     that which is most pleasing and acceptable to you.
Grant me now a moment of silence.
Keep me in your embrace through the night,
     give me quiet rest and your peace,
          now and forever. Amen.

BASED ON *IMITATION OF CHRIST* BY THOMAS à KEMPIS

FRIDAY MORNING

FORGIVENESS

Lord, show us your mercy and love,
and grant us your salvation.

LET LOVE RULE

Dear Lord,
in this time of sorrow and grief,
I find myself turning away when I need you most.
Help me to know that you are always by my side.
Help me to show a Christian attitude
even when I am least inclined.
Let kindness leave my mouth instead of harshness.
Let forgiveness be on my mind instead of anger.
Let peace be in my heart instead of pain.
Let faith rule my actions instead of resentment.
Let thankfulness shine through instead of self-pity.
Let love rule over hatred and apathy.
Lord, let your blessing guide this day and the next.
Amen.

ERIN VANDEN BUSCH, *Off-Campus*

EPHESIANS 4:30–5:2

Brothers and sisters:
Do not grieve the Holy Spirit of God,
  with which you were sealed for the day of redemption.
All bitterness, fury, anger, shouting, and reviling
  must be removed from you, along with all malice.
And be kind to one another, compassionate,
  forgiving one another
    as God has forgiven you in Christ.

So be imitators of God, as beloved children,
    and live in love,
  as Christ loved us and handed himself over for us
    as a sacrificial offering to God for a fragrant aroma.

ANTIPHON

A clean heart create for me, O God,
  and a steadfast spirit renew within me.

PSALM 51:3–4,12–13,14–15

Have mercy on me, O God, in your goodness;
  in the greatness of your compassion
    wipe out my offense.
Thoroughly wash me from my guilt
  and of my sin cleanse me.

A clean heart create for me, O God,
    and a steadfast spirit renew within me.
Cast me not out from your presence,
    and your Holy Spirit take not from me.
Give me back the joy of your salvation,
    and a willing spirit sustain in me.
I will teach transgressors your ways,
    and sinners shall return to you.

GLORY TO THE FATHER, and to the Son,
    and to the Holy Spirit,
as it was in the beginning, is now,
    and will be for ever. Amen.

CLOSING PRAYER

O Lord our God,
grant us grace to desire you with our whole heart,
that so desiring we may seek and find you,
and so finding you, may love you,
and loving you, may hate those sins
from which you have redeemed us. Amen.

ST. ANSELM

*T*hose who work without prayer—no matter how good the work, no matter how sincere the minister—soon dry up inside. They have nothing left to give. Or the work fails and they have no faith to sustain them, no perspective to encourage them. More importantly, real prayer changes us. Prayer delivers us from our own internal oppressions, the burdens we put on ourselves, the bitterness we carry, because it enables the inbreaking of God in our lives.

SISTER JOAN CHITTISTER, O.S.B.

FRIDAY EVENING

FORGIVENESS

Lord, show us your mercy and love,
and grant us your salvation.

SHOW ME YOUR LOVE, LORD

Lord, you have chosen me to be
    your faithful and humble servant,
        but I am weak; I fail.
Lord, you call me to be a light in
    this world and salt for your earth,
        but I am afraid; I rely only on my own strength.
Lord, you ask me to give of myself
    in love and service to all,
        but my motives are selfish; I want only for me.
Show me the power of your love, Lord.
Have mercy on me,
    and offer your forgiveness and healing. Amen.

CHRIS CHRISTENSEN, *Knott Hall*

LUKE 5:12-16

It happened there was a man full of leprosy
    in one of the towns where Jesus was;
and when he saw Jesus, he fell prostrate,
    pleaded with him, and said,
"Lord, if you wish, you can make me clean."

Jesus stretched out his hand, touched him, and said,
   "I do will it. Be made clean."
And the leprosy left him immediately.
Then he ordered him not to tell anyone,
   but "Go, show yourself to the priest
      and offer for your cleansing
   what Moses prescribed; that will be proof for them."
The report about him spread all the more,
   and great crowds assembled to listen to him
      and to be cured of their ailments,
   but he would withdraw to deserted places to pray.

ANTIPHON

Merciful and gracious is the Lord,
   slow to anger and abounding in kindness.

PSALM 103:1-4,8,10,12-13

Bless the LORD, O my soul;
   and all my being, bless his holy name.
Bless the LORD, O my soul,
   and forget not all his benefits.
He pardons all your iniquities,
   heals all your ills.
He redeems your life from destruction,
   crowns you with kindness and compassion.
Merciful and gracious is the LORD,
   slow to anger and abounding in kindness.

Not according to our sins does he deal with us,
    nor does he requite us according to our crimes.
As far as the east is from the west,
    so far has he put our transgressions from us.
As a father has compassion on his children,
    So the LORD has compassion on those who fear him.

GLORY TO THE FATHER, and to the Son,
    and to the Holy Spirit,
as it was in the beginning, is now,
    and will be for ever. Amen.

CLOSING PRAYER

O Lord my God,
thank you for bringing this day to a close;
    thank you for giving me rest in body and soul.
Your hand has been over me
    and has guarded and preserved me.
Forgive my lack of faith and any wrong
    I have done today,
        and help me to forgive all who have wronged me.
Let me sleep in peace under your protection,
    and keep me from all the temptations of darkness.
Into your hands I commend my loved ones
    and all who dwell in this house;
I commend to you my body and soul.
O God, your holy name be praised. Amen.

DIETRICH BONHOEFFER

SATURDAY MORNING

PEACE AND JUSTICE

Lord, you call us today to your service;
make us stewards of your many gifts.

A PRAYER FOR MISSION

Lord God,
Grant each of us
    seeking eyes to see your face,
    listening ears to hear your voice,
    outstretched hands to serve the poor,
    a loving heart to embrace the stranger,
    an honest tongue to bring justice to the world,
    and moving feet to go where peace is not yet found.
In the name of the Word made flesh
    because he dwells among us. Amen.

MERT HERSHBERGER, *1999 Alumnus*

ROMANS 12:17–21

Do not repay anyone evil for evil;
    be concerned for what is noble in the sight of all.
If possible, on your part, live at peace with all.
Beloved, do not look for revenge
    but leave room for the wrath;

for it is written, "Vengeance is mine,
    I will repay, says the Lord."
Rather, "If your enemy is hungry, feed him;
    if he is thirsty, give him something to drink;
for by so doing you will heap burning coals
    upon his head."
Do not be conquered by evil but conquer evil with good.

ANTIPHON

Faithfulness will spring up from the ground,
    and righteousness will look down from the sky.

PSALM 85:8-13

Let me hear what God the Lord will speak,
    for he will speak peace to his people,
        to his faithful, to those who turn
        to him in their hearts.
Surely his salvation is at hand for those who fear him,
    that his glory may dwell in our land.
Steadfast love and faithfulness will meet;
    righteousness and peace will kiss each other.
Faithfulness will spring up from the ground,
    and righteousness will look down from the sky.
The Lord will give what is good,
    and our land will yield its increase.
Righteousness will go before him,
    and will make a path for his steps.

GLORY TO THE FATHER, and to the Son,
    and to the Holy Spirit,
as it was in the beginning, is now,
    and will be for ever. Amen.

CLOSING PRAYER

Lord,
may you banish from the hearts of men and women,
    whatever might endanger peace.
May you transform each of us
    into witnesses of truth, justice, and love.
May you enlighten rulers of peoples
    so that they may guarantee
        and defend the great gift of peace.
May you enkindle the wills of all,
    so that we may overcome the barriers that divide,
cherish the bonds of mutual charity, understand others,
    and pardon those who have done us wrong.
By virtue of your action,
    may all peoples of the earth become
        as brothers and sisters,
and may the most longed-for peace blossom forth
    and reign forever. Amen.

POPE JOHN XXIII

SATURDAY EVENING

PEACE AND JUSTICE

Lord, you call us today to your service;
make us stewards of your many gifts.

PEOPLE OF PEACE

God of mercy and love,
you call us to be people of peace.
Teach us to be people of peace
in our words offered in comfort,
in our gestures given in welcome,
in our attitudes rendered in forgiveness
and acceptance.
Teach us to be people of peace
when the people we love are threatened.
Teach us to be people of peace
when we are disregarded or ignored.
Teach us to be people of peace
when violence, jealousy, and anger
stand between love, acceptance, and blessing.
Show us the way of peace in the example of Jesus,
the Son of Justice and Sign of Peace for all creation.
We ask this now and forever. Amen.

SISTER LOIS PAHA , O.P., *1989 Alumna*

ISAIAH 61:1-2A,10-11

The spirit of the Lord GOD is upon me,
>because the LORD has anointed me;
he has sent me to bring glad tidings to the poor,
>to heal the brokenhearted,
to proclaim liberty to the captives
>and release to the prisoners,
to announce a year of favor from the LORD
>and a day of vindication by our God.

I rejoice heartily in the LORD,
>in my God is the joy of my soul;
for he has clothed me with a robe of salvation
>and wrapped me in a mantle of justice,
like a bridegroom adorned with a diadem,
>like a bride bedecked with her jewels.
As the earth brings forth its plants,
>and a garden makes its growth spring up,
So will the Lord GOD make justice and praise
>spring up before all the nations.

ANTIPHON

The Lord raises up those who are bowed down.
>*The Lord loves the just.*

PSALM 146:6-10

The LORD God keeps faith forever,
    secures justice for the oppressed,
    gives food to the hungry.
The LORD sets captives free.
The LORD gives sight to the blind;
    the LORD raises up those who are bowed down.
The LORD loves the just;
    the LORD protects strangers.
The fatherless and the widow he sustains,
    but the way of the wicked he thwarts.
The LORD shall reign forever;
    your God, O Zion, through all generations.

GLORY TO THE FATHER, and to the Son,
    and to the Holy Spirit,
as it was in the beginning, is now,
    and will be for ever. Amen.

CLOSING PRAYER

God of Justice,
open our eyes to see you in the face of the poor.
Open our ears to hear you in the cries of the exploited.
Open our mouths to defend you in the public squares
    as well as in private deeds.
Remind us that what we do to the least ones,
    we do to you.
Amen.

CATHOLIC CAMPAIGN FOR HUMAN DEVELOPMENT

Praying with the Notre Dame Community

We often focus on key people, events, and places that hold meaning for us because they are associated with a significant insight or some point in our personal growth. They become important milestones and treasured experiences of the sacred and holy in our lives.

The prayers in this section fall into two categories, original compositions and favorite prayers. The original prayers, composed by students, staff, faculty, and alumni of the Notre Dame community, represent personal reflections about the growth, discernment, and self-awareness that characterize the journey through and beyond the college years.

The favorite prayers submitted by the Notre Dame community warranted selection because of their connection to how and why we pray at Notre Dame and because they either have become or are becoming part of the fabric of our prayer tradition on campus.

ORIGINAL PRAYERS ∾

COME, HOLY SPIRIT

I have a prayer to propose to you. It is very short,
only three words. They are opening words to the
wonderful prayer, *Veni, Sancte Spiritus*. In English,
of course, this is *"Come, Holy Spirit."*

When the Lord left his apostles, a very confused group,
he simply told them: "Don't worry, I will not leave you
orphans, I am sending you the Holy Spirit."

However, we have to call on him and those three simple
words, *"Come, Holy Spirit,"* bring us an infallible answer
to whatever problems we face, both to see what we
should do and to have the strength to do it."

Veni, Sancte Spiritus
"Come, Holy Spirit."

REV. THEODORE HESBURGH, C.S.C.

NOTRE DAME BLESSING

May the Golden Dome of Notre Dame shine upon you.
May the special sons and daughters of Notre Dame
    be forever.
May the spirit of Notre Dame bring you everlasting joy.
May the fires of Our Lady's Grotto always burn brightly
    in your life.

And may God, Country,
     and Notre Dame be a beacon
   on your journey. Amen.

RICK CHILDRESS, *Father of ND Grad*

SEMESTER BLESSING

May the Lord wake me each morning
   with energy and joy.
May the Lord bless my preparations,
   giving me an organized mind and enthusiastic heart.
May the Lord strengthen me each day
   with focus and perseverance.
May the Lord bless my classes,
   making me hungry to learn
   and eager to understand and remember.
May the Lord calm me each evening
   with peace and gentleness,
      blessing my studies with renewed motivation,
   my activities with joy and friendship,
     my conversations and relationships
     with untiring love.
May the Lord refresh me each night with health and rest,
   blessing my sleep with freedom from worry.
May my semester be fruitful,
  with my efforts bringing glory to the Lord,
and may I always know the joy and love of the Lord.
   Amen.

SHEILA PAYNE, *Cavanaugh Hall*

PRAYER OF A FRESHMAN

Lord,
help me in this time of transition,
    for with you I can do all things.
Help me to remember this as I begin my college life.
Help me to know that while it is difficult
    to leave family and friends behind,
        they will always be there for me.
Let me make the most of this blessing
    you have given me, this chance to be here
        at Notre Dame.
Give me the courage to be myself
    and to grow beyond my comforts.
Help me to try my best in academics,
    knowing that A's will sometimes be difficult to attain.
Most of all, Lord, help me to keep you first in my life.
    If I let you lead my way, I can never go wrong! Amen.

HOLLY PAVLICK, *Farley Hall*

*When one door of happiness closes,
    another one opens,
but we look so long at the closed door that we do
not see the one which has been opened for us.*

HELEN KELLER

EVERYTHING NEW

Dear Lord,
I am new here.
Every day I wake up in my new room,
    go to my new classes,
        try to make new friends.
But you are not new to me.
You have been here forever
    in this place called Notre Dame.
Your love and guiding presence
    are with me every day.
You are in the new roommate,
    the new professor,
        the new friend,
    the new me.
I know that you will be with me, Lord,
    during these next four years here.
Thank you for welcoming me, once again,
    into your home—my new home.
Amen.

MICHAEL VANDEN BOOM, *Dillon Hall*

FIRST YEAR STUDENT PRAYER

Lord,

please be with me as I enter a new stage in my life.

Grant me strength to accept the challenges that lay ahead,
  and to gracefully endure the trials.

Help me to fully appreciate and enjoy the gifts
  and experiences that await me.

Inspire me to fully share my talents and myself
    with the Notre Dame family,
      in the classroom, in the dorm, with my friends,
    and with you, Lord.

I ask that you watch over me as I study, work, play,
  and adjust to my new life while keeping in touch
    with my life at home.

Please grant me strength, wisdom, patience,
  and the gift of your love in all that I do this year. Amen.

LAURA WOLOHAN, *Pasquerilla East*

GROUP PRAYER

Dear God,

  in our hearts and all around,
help us to memorize the sound
  of the times we have prayed
    and gathered in your name.

Lord, help us to be always present to your call.

Help us to be stewards of your love,
  desiring to do your will in all things.

Lord, guide our stumbling feet
    and keep them on the path
  of honesty and truth.
As we walk this journey, encourage in us
    the ability and the desire to know you
      in every face, in every creature,
    in every experience and expression of creation
      we meet along the way. Amen.

KATHERINE TRAYNOR, KAREN CAVANAUGH, SARAH POPEK,
JENNIFER DISCHER, VALERIE AGUILAR, *Cavanaugh Hall*

A TEACHER'S PRAYER

God of wisdom and understanding,
help me as I strive to be a holy and sincere educator
  in the faith.
I ask that you inspire me to love my students,
    meeting them where they are
      and always seeking to understand.
Be with me inside and outside of the classroom,
    as I help my students to face the challenges
      and graces of growing up.
Grant me patience, courage, and enthusiasm,
    as I teach through my words and actions.
I thank you for granting me the privilege to influence
    young minds and hearts.
I ask all of these things, through Christ,
    our greatest teacher. Amen

KATHY MOTYKA, *2003 Alumna*

STUDENT'S PRAYER

O loving and merciful God,
　　my whole existence depends on you.
I ask you to send your Holy Spirit
　　　　into my heart and my mind.
Fill me with your grace
　　　　beyond my own personal strength,
　　so that I can dedicate the time and energy
　　　　that I need to study.
Give me the strength to resist distractions.
When I am studying by myself,
　　help me to remember
　　　　that you are my companion
　　and that I am never truly alone.
Help my professors to explain things clearly.
Help me to respect them.
Help me to pay attention and listen well in class.
Give me the courage to ask questions
　　when I don't understand.
Give me the humility to ask for help when I need it.
Help me to accept the grades that I get
　　after I have done all that I can do.
Give me a spirit of gratitude
　　for the privilege of studying at this University,
　　　　while most people in the world
　　will never have such a rare opportunity.

Help me to make the most
of the wonderful gifts
you have given me,
and to return them to you with generosity.
You have been with me through rough times in the past.
Help me to trust that you are here with me now.
Give me hope for the future,
and help me to trust that, whatever the future brings,
you are already there waiting for me
with your loving embrace.
I offer you this prayer through your Son,
my Lord and Savior Jesus Christ,
who lives and reigns with you, forever and ever. Amen.

REV. MICHAEL SIS, *1982 Alumnus*

A ROOMMATE'S PRAYER

Stay in my heart, Lord,
as I live and grow with my roommate.
Stay in my heart during the bad times,
that I may remain patient and remember the laughs.
Stay in my heart during the good times,
that I may not take them for granted.
Stay in my heart, Lord,
that in this troubling and confusing world,
I may always have a friend to come home to. Amen.

CHRISTOPHER STROTHER, *1998 Alumnus*

ND WEATHER

Lord,
as the year cools down, we feel it here through our coats,
 and so we are reminded of those with lesser coats.
As the big lake sends us snow falling sideways,
 we are reminded of our substantial shelter
  and of those without such sanctuary.
Rather than let the dark of winter be overwhelming,
 give us, O Lord, our own weather in our hearts,
  ever like the best day of spring.
Let us show that best day—
 warm, pleasant, and supportive
  in all things that are yours—
 to all who will see it. Amen.

FRANK BELLINI, *1971 Alumnus*

PRAYER AT THE GROTTO

Dear Mother,
it is good to be here with you,
 to come sit with you,
  to rest in your presence
 and leave all worries and anxieties in your lap.
Thank you for welcoming me with love.
Mother, my life is full with due dates, expectations,
 and faces of those I love.
I come to you with a full heart,
 so that you can lift me up and offer me to your Son.
I am filled with peace when I come here.

The candles, the people praying,
      the trees and tolling bells
   help me to clearly feel your love and prayers for me.
Please hold me close to you and place your Son
      in my heart. Amen.

CATHERINE BATESON, *Off-Campus*

TO THE CONTRARY

Dear Mary,
please help me
      to pray by listening,
      to obey by breaking new ground,
      to make an impression through humility,
      to show wisdom by citing right sources,
      to show strength by quiet steadfastness.

Please help me
      to attract by pointing beyond myself,
      to cry hardest for the sorrows of others,
      to share love without hoarding it,
      to accumulate truth without weaponizing it,
      to hope with trusting faith, not empty optimism.

Thank you for teaching me
      that these virtues can seem complex and contrary
            and yet are steps toward simplicity and wholeness.
      Amen.

BILL SCHMITT, *Kellogg Institute*

STILLNESS

Good and Gracious Lord,
amidst the ceaseless rush of days,
    the readings, the papers, the exams,
        I often feel overwhelmed.
As my life beyond this place beckons,
    I find myself realizing that I don't have all the answers.
I don't know which road to choose,
    or where my life will go from here.

In my quest for certainty,
    I am discovering that nothing is ever truly certain,
        except you.
When all my questions find no answers,
    you are the one truth,
        the core of stillness within my soul.

When the cares of the world distract me,
    help me to find your presence within,
        the pearl of calm amid the shifting sands.
Center me once more,
    so that I may face the tempests with renewed strength,
        with a purpose and support
    that come from you alone.

In you I find not certainty
    but understanding,
and in that understanding
    a perfect peace. Amen.

KIRSTIN KRUEGER, *Badin Hall*

A PRAYER FOR THE GRACE OF ATTENTIVENESS

O God, Creator, Sustainer, and Redeemer,
    our waking hours are often so hurried, hectic,
        and filled with responsibilities
    that we fail to experience the wonder and mystery
        with which you have imbued our lives.
We overlook the simple joys,
    ignore your unexpected intrusions of Grace,
        and at times make little room
    for sacred silence and stillness.
Grant that we may pause, if only briefly,
        to listen attentively
    for your "still, small voice"
        whispering words of comfort,
    singing songs of joy, and reminding us
        of that most *elegant truth*
    revealed on the first Easter morn—
        that love conquers death
    and in Christ all things are made new.
May this *Good News* be our comfort and strength,
    this day and always.
We ask this in the name
        of the one in whose *Way* we walk,
    Jesus Christ, our Lord. Amen.

HUGH PAGE, *Theology Professor*

SATURDAY NIGHT AT THE LIBRARY

I need to find that balance, Lord,
>between studying and spending time with my friends.

You have blessed me so greatly
>that I am able to attend this University.

And for this I thank you.

But help me to remember that I am here
>for more than an academic education.

While I am surrounded by future authors,
>philosophers, scientists, and engineers,
>>let me appreciate that I am also surrounded
>by people who can share their lives
>>with me right now—
>people I can laugh with, learn from and love.

These people, my friends, will be a part of my life forever.

Help me to see your presence in them
>and to focus on my relationships with them,
>>and with you.

Do not let me ignore the wonderful gifts
>you have given me in others.

Before I spend another Saturday night at the library,
>help me to remember that 10 years from now,
>>my joy and happiness will lie
>in my friends and loved ones,
>>not in my transcript. Amen.

MARY PLUMB, *1996 Alumna*

THE OBSERVATORY

*"The heavens declare the glory of God,
and the firmament proclaims his handiwork."*

PSALM 19:1

O Lord,
what started out as homework
    has became a moment of grace.
Now, visiting the observatory is something I love.
As I admire the pure beauty of the heavens,
    the sheer incomprehensible nature of your creation,
    your breathtaking kingdom of sun, moon, and stars,
    the magnificent cosmos shaped by your awesome hand,
I am nearly overwhelmed by it all.
It has a way of making me feel
    quite small and insignificant.
But gazing into space makes it possible
    to sense your Divine Presence
    and to feel your peace gracing the night sky.
As I study the stars,
    much like the shepherds and magi of old,
    I cannot help but be more aware of your power—
    immense as it is—
    and feel more connected to you.
To visit the observatory is to glimpse your glory. Amen.

MATT PLASKA, *Keough Hall*

PRAYER BEFORE STUDYING

Heavenly Father,
thank you for the opportunity to study
    at this University of Our Lady.
Help me to realize that my work here is not in vain;
       that in learning about my world,
    I will better know the workings of your creation.
Send your Holy Spirit upon me
    to increase my strength, patience, and fortitude,
       so that this time will help me to grow
    in wisdom and understanding.
In Jesus' name, I pray. Amen.

AARON KHERIATY, *1999 Alumnus*

PRAYER BEFORE AN EXAM

Dear Lord,
sometimes I feel a little strange praying to you
    because of an exam.
It doesn't really seem all that significant
    when you consider the "big picture."
But right now, the test looms so large
    that it is all I can see before me.
I pray to you for three things:
      —the strength to handle the pressure I feel,
      —the confidence to feel secure in my knowledge
        and preparation,
      —and the ability to keep an appropriate perspective
        on it all.

Help me to keep in mind
    what is really important,
   even as I focus all of my time and energy
    on this test in the immediate future.

DANA PARISI, *1995 Alumna*

PRAYER FOR MODERATION

Lord,
you know what is best for me; I belong to you.
All that I am and all that has been given me
   is gift from you.
If I choose to drink, please help me…
   to care for my body,
   to drink responsibly and conscientiously,
   to drink to celebrate the blessings of life and friendship,
    rather than to escape or abuse.
If I choose not to drink, please help me…
   to withstand any pressure or ridicule,
   to remain confident in your strength,
   to be at peace with my decision.
May I act in ways that respect others and myself.
Above all, grant me the grace to model Jesus, your Son,
   that I too may be filled with joy and act with love.
Amen.

MIKE SENA, *Zahm Hall.*

PRAYER ABOUT DATING

Divine Lover,
you created me to love and be loved.
I desire this love intensely and search for it eternally.
Bless my search for this love as I date.
May I always remember that only you
    can fulfill my every desire,
        and that love is an active decision.
I ask you to be present and central in my relationships.
Keep my focus on growing closer to you
    by growing to love another.
May my love for another mirror your love for me.
Guide me away from the temptations of the flesh
    and towards purity.
Allow me to trust,
    and help me to always remain trustworthy.
Lead me to desire what is best for those I date
    over anything I want from them
        and from our relationship.
Remind me always that you have a plan for me,
    greater than I could ever imagine.
In your name I pray. Amen.

JOHN SENGENBERGER, *Morrissey Hall*

THE GIFT OF SEXUALITY

Loving God, source of all truth and strength,
    help me to come to know you more fully
        through a greater awareness of myself
    and those closest to me.

I know that through loving others,
   I can come to a greater awareness
      of your presence
   by entering into the challenges and joys
      of a healthy relationship.
Be with me as I strive to be open
   to your great mystery in my life
   and in the lives of those I love.
As I try to understand the great gift of my sexuality,
   help me to be true to what is deepest in my heart.
Give me the patience to be still and listen
   for your whisper.
Then, help me to express this gift, with all of its mystery,
   in accord with what is true within me.
Grant me the strength to resist the pressure from others
   when it is not in keeping with your will for me.
May my need for emotional intimacy
   not overshadow an honest decision
      about what I want to say physically.
I know that in choosing to remain true to myself,
   I am also being truthful to you
      and those I love so dearly.
Gracious God,
   be with me in times of doubt.
Help me to express my true giftedness
   in all of my choices and actions. Amen.

DARRELL PAULSEN, *Campus Ministry*

PRAYER BEFORE COMPETITION

Dear Lord,
it would not be fair of me to pray for victory today,
 because my competitors are probably asking for the same.
So instead...
I pray that you will help me to be alert, to be focused,
 and to perform to the best of my ability.
I pray that the competition is fair, the judges are just,
 and all are free from cheating.
I pray for the safety of my teammates, my competitors,
 and myself both today and in the future.
And, I pray that I will learn something today
 that will help me improve and
  perform better in the days ahead.
In your name I pray. Amen.

COLLEEN WALSH, *Lewis Hall*

PRAYER TO PLAY FAIR
IN THE GAME OF LIFE

Dear Lord,
 in the struggle that goes on through life,
we ask for a field that is fair,
 a chance that is equal with all the strife,
  the courage to strive and to dare;
and if we should win, let it be by the code,
 with our faith and our honor held high;
and if we should lose, let us stand by the road
 and cheer as the winners go by.

KNUTE ROCKNE

PRAYER OF AN ATHLETE

Most Powerful and Gracious God,
    you never stop opening my eyes to your truth.

By your wonderful grace,
    you have given me a body, mind and spirit . . .
        alive with energy, motivation, and dedication.
I have come to love the thrill of competition,
    the excitement of success,
        and the joy of sharing it all with my teammates.

Your greatest gift to me, through these years of training,
        practice and competition,
    has also been the hardest
        to accept . . . HUMILITY.

You blessed me with abilities and talents
    and encouraged me to use them,
    but for every moment of victory
        I have known five moments of defeat.

And in these moments I am reminded
    that my strength lies not within me, but in you.
Humble my heart, Lord.
Never let me forget to praise you above all else,
    so that my entire being may be purified of pride
        and always mindful of the unending gifts of grace
    that spill forth from you. Amen.

KEARA COUGHLIN, *Pangborn Hall*

PRAYER FOR MIDSHIPMEN AND CADETS

Lord,
I often wonder why I am doing what I am doing.
Early morning runs, weekend field exercises,
    uniforms that don't protect
        against the bitter January cold…
No one else has these rules!
What does all of this mean?
Parents who are proud,
    friends who challenge me
        to think about the moral issues,
    an opportunity for an education,
        a call to serve.
Yes, Lord…
I believe you are calling me to serve.
I believe that your guidance and spirit
    have brought me to this point in my life.
As I face each day, and look ahead
    to commissioning and life as an officer,
I call upon you for continued guidance
    as I strive to do your will.
Help me to remember I am a Christian first
        before all else,
    that I may honor your name in my bearing,
        my language, and my lifestyle.
Grant me courage to honor my convictions,
    the strength to lead, and the humility to follow.

May I be just in command,
   compassionate in counsel,
      and trustworthy in word and performance.
Allow me wisdom in decision-making,
   and patience to let myself grow
      through success and failure.
Make me choose the harder right
      instead of the easier wrong,
   and never to be content with a half-truth
      when the whole can be won.
Loving God,
   I trust in your mercy and your grace.
Be near me as I continue my journey,
   that I may remain ever close to you
      in the challenge to come.
Amen.

TRISH POWERS, *1998 Alumna*

---

*What is good has been explained to you;
this is what Yahweh asks of you, only this:
to act justly, to love tenderly and to walk humbly
with your God.*   MICAH 6:8

I *did not know then,*
as I know now,
this quality of in-loveness
when we see individuals
as God sees them,
in all their beauty;
and all the earth
seems transformed.
Suddenly all around me
the world has lightened,
the fog has lifted,
and the air has cleared,
and one understands
what we are capable
of becoming
and how many ways
we are indeed
the image of God.

DOROTHY DAY

CADET PRAYER

Dear Lord,
please show me the way as I pursue
    my vocation of service,
        a service to my country
    as a future commissioned officer in the armed forces.
I ask for your blessing as I learn the art of leadership
    and cultivate other talents needed to succeed,
        not only in the military, but in life as well.
Grant all cadets and midshipmen
        the strength of conviction
    to stand up for what they know to be morally right,
        against the ridicule of others
        and pressures of the moment.
May I take all that I can from my Notre Dame experience,
    making me a better cadet, a better leader,
        and most of all, a better person. Amen.

SHANE LARSON, *Alumni Hall*

PRAYER FOR SELF-ACCEPTANCE

Lord,
I come before you ready to fill myself
    with your transforming love.
Thank you for the gift of life,
    and help me to recognize and appreciate
        the talents and graces you have given me.
Sometimes, Lord, your blessings
    become distorted in my eyes,
        and I seek futilely to change the person I am.
Help me to have the confidence to accept myself
    as the person you have created
        and the wisdom to truly love myself
    as the wonderful creation that I am—
        a unique individual, a work of art
        with your signature upon my soul. Amen.

LESLIE PECHKUROW, *Lyons Hall*

DISAPPOINTMENT

Lord,
I did not get what I wanted this time.
It is difficult to deal with the disappointment.
I need your help.
I know that I must keep things in perspective.
Everything happens for a reason,
    and I should count the many blessings
        that have brought me here.
But, this feels far from insignificant to me right now.

Give me the strength to trust
     in your plan for me
  and to recognize that this disappointment
     will soon become a mere crack in the pavement,
  a speck on a greater horizon. Amen.

KATIE WELCH, *Cavanaugh Hall*

MADE IN YOUR IMAGE

Loving God,
  my eating habits are out of control.
No one here knows about my problem, and I feel so alone.
I am surrounded by community,
  but I am scared to let people see the real me.
I am not as confident as everyone thinks I am,
  and I crave emotional intimacy.

Everywhere I go there is a voice in my head,
  telling me I am not good enough.
At the dining hall, the Rock, even walking to class,
  I compare my body to the bodies
    of so many other women
  who seem to have it all together.
Please remind me that I am your child,
  made in your image and likeness.
Please help me to know that I am good enough
  just the way you made me.
Give me the courage to open up
  to the wonderful people you have placed in my life
    here at Notre Dame. Amen.

ERICA BOVE, *Badin Hall*

COURAGE

Dear Lord,
thank you for blessing me with courage—
    courage to try new things,
        in spite of the fear of embarrassment;
    courage to undertake challenges,
        even if I cannot conceive the outcome;
    courage to articulate my beliefs,
        knowing there may be opposition.

Lord, I have been given the opportunity
    to meet new people,
  to experience new sights, and to voice my opinions.
I have faced obstacles along the way,
but I thank you for giving me the courage to continue—
    to know that challenges make me stronger,
    to know that fear is sometimes inevitable,
    to know that in every situation you stand beside me,
        offering reassurance when I doubt.

Thank you Lord, for giving me courage—
    courage to live, courage to experience,
        and courage to pray.
Amen.

KRISTIANNA SANTOS, *Pangborn Hall*

PRAYER WITHOUT BOUNDARIES

O kind and gracious God,
I pray these words knowing
      that you hear the meditations of my heart.
Your goodness and loving kindness
    calm my spirit and urge me to stay still,
       resting in the warmth of your divine presence.
Teach me this day to embrace all of life.
Help me to see you in every person I meet
    and in every road I travel.
Open my eyes to the seamless beauty of this world,
    crafted to reflect the splendor and wonder
      of your divine life.
Help me to live as Christ lived,
    accepting in love every experience that comes my way.
I commit this day to embrace all—fearlessly.
You are my God and I love you.
Because of you, I am not afraid.
Because of you, I am Christ to the world. Amen.

CHANDRA JOHNSON, *Assistant Director, Cross Cultural Ministry*

IN MEMORY OF DAD

Dear Lord,
    we mourn our dad daily, all in new and different ways.
We miss his smile and his scowl,
    his laugh along with his temper.
We miss his courage and resilience, his wit and kind heart.
We miss every part of Dad; it's what made him ours.

Heavenly Father, I ask you these things:
Help me to cope with the death of my father.
Help me to find solace in your wisdom.
Grant me the strength I need to be there for my family.
Grant them the strength they will need to be there for me.
Allow me to mourn, to cry, to be angry,
    and to question "Why?"
Allow me to understand that he will suffer no longer.
Let me not dwell on the events he will miss.
Let me remember how much he enjoyed days past.
Forgive me for not telling him I loved him enough.
Forgive me for the times I fall below his expectations of me.
I will cherish his memory, his name,
    and all he instilled in our family.
I will take pride in the fact that I am who I am
    because of him.
I know he will forever be in my corner,
    watching over my family.

I know I am a better person
  simply for having him in my life.
I pray that he know
  how much I love and miss him.
I pray that I never take for granted what he has meant
  to my mother, my family, and me.
Lord, I ask this in your name. Amen.

PAT McGARRY, *Zham Hall*

CELEBRATION OF DIFFERENCES

Lord,
In a world forever shrinking,
  I come face to face with people
    who are different from me in every way.
Help me to see these people as my brothers and sisters
  with the same need to belong, to create, to grow,
    to be free, to be loved.
Dispel any fear I may have towards them,
  and allow my arms and my heart to surround them
    with acceptance and caring. Amen.

DAVID SCHIESHER, *1980 Alumnus*

TOWARD A SPIRIT OF INCLUSION AT NOTRE DAME

We thank you, God, source of all holiness
    for creating this place we call home
  and for blessing it with life
    in such abundance and diversity.
You have created humans of many colors
  and have blessed us with the birth of many cultures.
You have created us and blessed us
  with unique perspectives
    of what it means to be women and men
  called to be in relationship to you and one another.
Yet, in our sinful, broken, human condition,
  we are hindered in our attempt to be one with you
  and with one another.
Open all minds, loving God,
  that all your children will come to understand
    the unity of which you are both source and goal.
Invite all people to an ever greater appreciation
  of that marvelous diversity
    which has its source in you.
Open our heart that we might be moved
  to act with courage
    against ignorance and injustice.
Because we welcome and value lesbian and gay members
  of our Notre Dame community,
    help us to be an inclusive people.

By our Baptism and life in Christ,
    draw all of us into communion
        and community with one another,
    and guide our steps as we seek
        to find our way back to you.
We make this prayer in the name of Jesus,
    your son and our brother who lives and reigns
    with you and among the human family. Amen.

REV. THOMAS DOYLE, C.S.C.

A SEMESTER ABROAD

Loving God,
be with me as I leave Notre Dame for a semester abroad.
Support me as I give up the comfort
    of this beautiful place
        and supportive community.
When my faith is challenged,
    remind me that my Notre Dame education
        is part of who I have become.
May it nurture me to do your work
    and to grow in a foreign place.
I thank you for the blessing of a semester abroad,
    a chance to grow in wisdom and faith.
Grant me rich opportunities to see more
    of the world you have created.
When I return, encourage me to be a light to others
    in the sharing of my experiences. Amen.

LAURA HOFFMAN, *Lyons Hall*

PRAYER FOR INTERNATIONAL STUDENTS

Lord,
bless those students who have traveled far
from their home countries
to join the Notre Dame family.
May they find reminders of their homelands
and people eager to share their culture.
May they feel welcomed to this community,
and surrounded by friends to comfort them
in times of need.
May you guide them on their educational journeys
and give them happiness in all endeavors.
May Notre Dame become like a second home for them.
Lord, bless all International Students.
Give them peace, keep them safe during their travels,
and protect them while they are here with us. Amen.

CECILIA LESMES, *Lewis Hall*

SERVICE

Lord,
I left to serve and I was served.
I went to save and I was saved.
I went to teach and I was taught.
I went to love and I was loved.
I went to help and I was helped.
I went to be compassionate
    and others were compassionate toward me.
I went to help the humble and I was humbled.
I went to mend the broken and I was broken.
I am still me, but I went with a heart of stone,
    and now I have a heart of love.
Amen.

RITA MORGAN, *Badin Hall*

*I am part and parcel of the whole
and cannot find God
apart from the rest of humanity.*

GANDHI

JPW

Lord,
we give you thanks this weekend
    for the wonderful blessings
        you have bestowed upon us,
    especially the beauty of this place
        we know as Notre Dame.
You provide us with the understanding to do your will
    in our daily acts and the strength to carry it out.
It is your spirit and love that shine in us,
    brightening our path.
We thank you for the extraordinary people
        you have shared with us
    who guide us on our journey here at Notre Dame:
our rectors who provide us with help and guidance;
our professors who nourish our hunger for knowledge
    and challenge us with each class;
our friends who join us on this journey and
    share not only their time, but also their hearts;
our parents and guardians who give us our roots,
    provide us with abundant love,
        and give of themselves unconditionally.
They all allow our journey
    to be full of your love and joy.
Heavenly Father,
    we ask that you continue to light our path
    into lives that will fulfill your will.

Let us open our hearts
    to those around us
  and never forget that you are always with us.
We pray through Christ our Lord. Amen.

KATHYA VALDEZ, *Welsh Family Hall*

A SENIOR'S PRAYER

God of Guiding Light and Love,
your presence during these years
    has enlivened and comforted me.
Through your gentle care,
    I have grown and experienced so much.
It was easy to feel you around me
    in the beauty and fellowship of this place.
As my future presents itself,
    calm my worries and fears,
    remain by my side,
    direct my path as our journey together continues.
With you I continue on,
    expectant and excited
      for the life awaiting me. Amen.

FAITH BACHNER-REIMER, *Pasquerilla East*

R.A.'S PRAYER

Good and Gracious God,
I come before you to celebrate the legacy
    of women and men who came before me.
I come thanking you for visionaries who imagined
    this place and faithful faculty and staff who give it life.
I remember all those whose work and witness
    have brought me to this moment.
And I know that I am not alone.
I come before you to celebrate the privilege
    of serving under the mantle of Our Lady.
I come thanking you for the residents
    and the rich and rugged stories of their lives.
I recall the many blessed and trying encounters
    that punctuated this day and night...
But I know that I am not alone.
I come before you with humble recognition
    that I do not have all the answers; and yet,
I come with confidence that you will empower me
    through community to be better
        than I thought I could be.
I recognize your grace that transforms me
    into the person you have called me to be.
And I know that I am not alone.

Through the watchful care
    and intercession of Notre Dame,
        Our Mother,
    send your Spirit…
    that I might see you in this ministry,
    that I might be you in this ministry,
    that I might never be alone. Amen.

HEATHER RAKOCZY, *Pangborn Hall Rector*

A PRAYER AT GRADUATION

Dear Lord,
I thank you and praise you
    for the strength and wisdom you have granted me,
    gifts that have helped me reach this day.
I know that graduation is not an ending, but a beginning,
    and I ask the Holy Spirit's continued guidance
    as I take the next step in my life.
Help me to remember your Son's words,
    "Much is expected from the person
        to whom much is given."
I have been given the great gift
    of a Notre Dame education.
Help me to use this gift to do your will.
Amen.

AMY SCHILL, *Pasquerilla East*

PRAYING PSALM 139

Lord,
You know me inside and out,
    you are aware of every action and thought.
You chart my movements, my habits;
    before I say a word you know it.
You enfold me in your loving arms,
    your touch reassures me always.
I am in awe of your knowledge;
    your insight is beyond my comprehension.

Your spirit finds me anywhere,
    I cannot escape your presence.
You are ubiquitous in time and space;
    past and present, height and depth.
You accompany me to the
    farthest reaches of sea and sky,
Though I seek to stray,
    you show me the path of life.
You permeate my inner darkness
    with your flame of undying love.

It was you who shaped my soul,
    who molded me before my birth.
How can I help but praise you
    who made me so wonderfully!
You know every facet of me,
    even those hidden within.

You alone directed the
    mystery of my becoming.
You know what will be
    in my days to come,
    until I see you face to face. Amen.

KIRSTIN KRUEGER, *Badin Hall*

GRACE EMERGING

O Lord,
    you know me perfectly;
        help me to know you more.
You are for seeing through hope and wonder...
    past my vision of the ordinary,
        the flash of familiarity in the stranger,
    the sound of an unknown voice intended for me.
O Lord,
    you know me perfectly;
    help me to know you more. Amen.

LEONARD DELORENZO, *Zahm Hall*

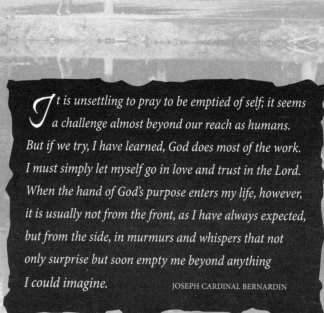

*I*t is unsettling to pray to be emptied of self; it seems
a challenge almost beyond our reach as humans.
But if we try, I have learned, God does most of the work.
I must simply let myself go in love and trust in the Lord.
When the hand of God's purpose enters my life, however,
it is usually not from the front, as I have always expected,
but from the side, in murmurs and whispers that not
only surprise but soon empty me beyond anything
I could imagine.   JOSEPH CARDINAL BERNARDIN

VOCATION PRAYER

God, my destiny and my hope,
I put my trust in you and in your son, Jesus Christ.
You know where I am meant to go.
You know what type of person I am called to be.
And most importantly, you know how
    I can build up your Kingdom.
Therefore, this day I lift up my worries, doubts and fears
    about my vocation to you.
Guide me, as you have all men and women
    who have struggled to be faithful to your call.
May these holy men and women serve
    as models for my formation.
They knew, as I know now,
    that you are the way to the light of truth.
I will never be lost in the darkness of uncertainty
    as long as I follow your light.
As I continue to follow the path set before me,
    I pray for the courage to embrace the challenges
        of knowing and accepting my vocation. Amen.

JAKE GREINER, *Old College*

THE CALLING

Lord,
continue to call; persist in your calling to me.
I often do not hear you,
  because I ignore you.
I often do not hear you,
  because I give in to temptation.
I often do not hear you,
      because I fail to make the effort—
    effort required to follow the path you have laid out for me,
    effort to see the eyes of Jesus in every face I meet,
    effort to love others as myself,
    effort to come closer to you and your way.
Forgive these failures to hear your call.
Help me to continually think of those in need,
    rather than being caught up
      in the race to gain material possessions.
Lead me toward being the best person I can be,
    the only person you are calling me to be.

Lord, this I pray. Amen.

ROBERT MUNDT, *1996 Alumnus*

PRAYER FOR GUIDANCE AND DIRECTION

Loving God,
I give you thanks for this day you have give me.
I ask that your Son be with me.
I ask that your Spirit be with me.
Guide and direct my thoughts and my actions,
    so that others may see the love
  that Christ has given to everyone in me.
Help me to be aware of the needs
    of those around me,
and give me the courage to share your love
    with everyone I meet.
In Jesus' name. Amen.

RICHARD WARNER, *Power Plant Controls*

I am only one, but I am one.
I cannot do everything,
but I can do something.
What I can do, I ought to do,
And what I ought to do,
by the grace of God, I will do.

TOM DOOLEY

THERE IS GOD

Ubi caritas et amor, Deus ibi est.
Where charity and love are found,
    there is God.

In every flake of snow,
    in every grain of sand—
        there is God.
In the stout and stoic strength of our brother, the mountain,
    in the swift and sure vigor of our sister, the sea—
        there is God.
When cold winds whip the head,
    when warm breezes brush the face—
        there is God.
In the darkest hour of the blackest night,
    in the brightest light of a golden afternoon—
        there is God.
When we are uplifted by the joys of victory,
    when we are wracked by the sorrows of defeat—
        there is God.
When we are surrounded by companions,
    when we are isolated in solitude and loneliness—
        there is God.
In the laughter of a friend,
    in the smile of a stranger—
        there is God.
God is always there.

Lord, grant that we may always
    walk with you
      and that we may have the peace, joy,
        and love that is your countenance. Amen.

JARED SYLVESTER, *Zahm Hall*

GRACE FOR THE JOURNEY

Hail Mary, full of grace,
I long to walk like you—
    to accept the journey on which God has called me
      with trust and a calm heart,
    to acknowledge my fears but then set them aside
      and follow God's call with a resounding yes,
    to proceed gently and with confidence,
      greeting others with warmth along the way.

Holy Mary, Mother of God,
I seek your soul in the landscape around me
    and discern your voice in my fellow travelers.
I forge ahead, praying unceasingly
    for the grace that clings to your very being. Amen.

LAURA MERRITT BIRD, *1996 Alumna*

PRAYER FOR BLESSING
AT ENGAGEMENT

Gentle, loving Lord,
I come before you in thanksgiving and wonder.
You have given me one who will walk with me
    for the rest of my life.
Words cannot tell;
    my heart at rest before you speaks silent thanksgiving.

But Lord, I am afraid.
You know me well, and I have seen
    my own lack of trust that this love can endure,
    and many times I have not let such love enter my life.
Now I am challenged to make a gift of myself,
    always to be present, never to leave.
This same gift is promised me.

Give me your help, Lord, to accept the challenge,
    and to return in love the great gift
        you have given us both. Amen.

REV. WILLIAM SIMMONS, C.S.C.

PRAYER FOR
EXPECTING PARENTS

Loving Creator,
we thank you for blessing us with new life and hope.
We are humbled by the life growing through our love
    and give thanks for the miracle of creation.
As the birth of our child approaches,
    we ask for continued health and strength.
May our minds, hearts, and bodies be prepared
    for the joys and challenges ahead.
We ask for confidence.
As we face the unknown, may we learn to trust ourselves
    and each other more deeply,
        knowing that you will guide us.
We ask for patience.
Through sleepless nights and days of struggle,
    may we remember that life reveals itself
        in unexpected ways.
We ask for guidance.
Continue to teach and lead us
    as we strive to raise our child in your name.
Above all, we ask, each and every day,
    for the ability to appreciate the new life
        we have created through your love. Amen.

MIKE AND WENDY SCHMIEDELER, *1994 alumni*

EVENING MEAL BLESSING

Loving God,
you know the hungers that we experience each day…
    our hunger for food and drink,
    for quiet and comfort,
    for shelter and community,
    for a home and people with whom to share it.
Lord, you know our hunger for love
    and our hunger for you.
Tonight we give you thanks for the many ways
you have nourished and satisfied our needs.
We give you thanks for this food,
    this time we will share,
        and those who have brought us together.
Loving God,
you are our hunger and our satisfaction.
Bless our food; bless us. Amen.

REV. THOMAS DOYLE, C.S.C.

PRAYER FOR GOSPEL LIVING
IN THE SPIRIT OF THE COMMUNITY
OF SANT'EGIDIO

Dear Lord, you give us the Word of God
    and ask us to make it the center of our lives.
Help us to listen to the Word daily
    discovering in it the challenge
        to live more authentically the life of discipleship.

O Lord, teach us to pray,
    that we might learn
        to better love you and one another.
Dear Lord, you do not call us servants, but friends.
Just as you offer us friendship,
    teach us to daily seek the poor,
        the imprisoned, the elderly, the forgotten,
    and to offer them the same friendship.
Help us to remember that your Gospel
    cannot be lived far from these least
        of our brothers and sisters.
May we follow the example of St. Francis,
    who was not afraid to kiss the leper,
        and who gave away his riches
    for the sake of building your kingdom.
Dear Lord, there is much conflict in our world.
Strengthen us to be servants of peace,
    seeking dialogue and reconciliation
        instead of violence and war.
May we learn to live as one family,
    embracing differences of nation,
        culture, and religion,
    and healing division wherever it exists. Amen.

KELLY RICH, *2002 Alumna*

IN THANKSGIVING

Loving God.
I praise and honor you
    as the one who directs my life.
I thank you for your son, Jesus,
    sign of your grace and mercy.
I thank you for all you have done for me
    and for all you are about to do in my life.
I thank you for my family and for my Notre Dame family.
Continue to bless us as you see fit.
I pray that you look down on this world
    and give us peace.
Show us how to love one another
    and do the things that are pleasing to you.
Amen.

DENISE McEWEN, *Building Services*

GOD'S SUFFERING SERVANT

My Lord,
with grace and humility you taught me how
    to accept the role of Suffering Servant.
You remind me that for those to whom much is given,
    much is expected in return.
Grant me this strength of purpose in serving others.
Remind me that your Spirit dwells
      in each person I encounter.

Allow me to embrace your example
    as I wash their feet,
  knowing they can more easily continue
    their journey toward you.
Finally Lord, open my mind and heart to the wisdom
  gained by giving.
I ask this through the power of Christ,
  my loving Redeemer. Amen.

TIM CALLAN, *Zahm Hall*

IN THE AFTERMATH OF 9/11

Lord God,
We feel the insecurities of this world at war.
Calm our hearts, and remind us anew
  of our dependence on you
    and your personal love for each one of us.
Send forth your Spirit to guide our personal decisions
  and our faithful response to your call to love.
Give wisdom to our world leaders
  and guide those who serve in the military.
Grant us the peace
    that only you can give:
  the peace that is fruit of a just world.
May your peace reign in our hearts and in our world
  and guide us to choose pathways of love.
We pray in the name of Jesus
  and through the intercession of Notre Dame,
    our Mother. Amen.

CAROLYN SHERMAN, *Campus Ministry*

PRAYER FOR VICTIMS OF WAR

Dear Lord,
>   make me grateful for the blessings of family
>>   and the safety and comforts of home.
>
> Keep me mindful of the sufferings
>   of those trying to live amid the violence of war.
>
> I pray that you will show them your grace
>   in the little things around them,
>>   such as the birth of a new baby,
>>   the marriage of two people,
>>   the love between family members and friends.
>
> I pray most of all that you can comfort them
>   in their moments of fear
>>   and in their times of grieving,
>   so that they may know you
>>   and find strength in your love. Amen.

NATASHA MIKHA, *Lyons Hall*

PRAYER FOR PRISONERS

Lord God,
> I ask your blessing today
>   on all your beloved women, men, and young people
>>   who are behind prison bars.
>
> In your mercy forgive their transgressions
>>   as you have always forgiven mine,
>   and help those whom they have harmed in any way.

Give all prisoners hope
    when they are tempted to despair
        and, if it is your will,
    return them soon to the arms
        of those whom they love.
I ask this in the name of your son, Jesus Christ,
    a fellow prisoner. Amen

REV. THOMAS MCNALLY, C.S.C.

ABANDONMENT INTO GOD'S ARMS

Loving God,
I offer you my pain
    and trust you for healing.
I offer you my tears
    and trust you for comfort.
I offer you my darkness
    and trust you for light.
I offer you my loneliness
    and trust you for companionship.
I offer you my despair
    and trust you for eternal hope.
I offer you my death
    and trust you for new life.
I offer you all that I have in this world
    and trust you for a new heaven and new earth.
I offer you nothing
    and trust you for all. Amen.

MERT HERSHBERGER, *1999 Alumnus*

COMMUNION

Lord Jesus,
Help me to see each person I am with today
    as a gift from you.
That I may love simply,
    let your Holy Spirit keep me mindful of the miracle
        that is our life together.

Thank you, Jesus, for the gift of Eucharist.
Through the miracle of your presence among us,
        each person I see today
    is no less a gift than is your precious Body and Blood.

We share in this same Eucharist the world over.
By your mercy, help us to make today
    a living communion with you
    through our communion with each other. Amen.

PROFESSOR DAVID A. SMITH, *Psychology*

*T*hou who are at home
   deep in my heart,
help me to join you deep in my heart.

THE TALMUD

TAKEN AND BLESSED,
BROKEN AND SHARED

Dear God,
I reflect upon the Eucharistic prayer,
    one of the most powerful prayers of the Mass.
Bread and wine become your Body and Blood,
    and I realize that we, too,
        are taken, blessed, broken, shared.
You took us, God—
    chose us to be your people,
        to be an example and to follow Jesus.
You blessed us, God—
    gifted us with loving families,
        talents, and treasures beyond imagination.
We are broken, God—
    by days when it is too difficult to go on,
        when skies seem forever gray.
But we share, God,
        in your kingdom, in your glory,
    and we know that you are with us
        in all that we do.
Thank you for being with us.
Thank you for choosing us,
    blessing us, helping us to fix what is broken,
        allowing us to share at your banquet. Amen.

CHRISTY LINDEMANN, *Farley Hall*

*T*he fruit of silence is prayer
The fruit of prayer is faith
The fruit of faith is love
The fruit of love is service
The fruit of service is peace

BLESSED MOTHER TERESA OF CALCUTTA

FAVORITE PRAYERS

ROAD AHEAD

My Lord God,
I have no idea where I am going.
I do not see the road ahead of me.
I cannot know for certain where it will end.
Nor do I really know myself,
  and the fact that I think that I am following your will
    does not mean that I am actually doing so.
But I believe that the desire to please you
  does in fact please you.
And I hope that I have that desire
  in all that I am doing.
I hope that I will never do anything
  apart from that desire.
And I know that if I do this,
  you will lead me by the right road
    though I may know nothing about it.
Therefore will I trust you always
  though I may seem lost and in the shadow of death.
I will not fear, for you are ever with me,
  and you will never leave me to face my perils alone.

THOMAS MERTON

DAY BY DAY

Thank you, Lord Jesus Christ,
for all the benefits and blessings
which you have given me,
for all the pains and insults
which you have borne for me.
Merciful Friend, Brother and Redeemer,
may I know you more clearly,
love you more dearly,
and follow you more nearly, day by day.

ST. RICHARD OF CHICHESTER

ST. PATRICK'S BREASTPLATE

Christ with me, Christ before me,
Christ behind me, Christ in me,
Christ beneath me, Christ above me,
Christ on my right, Christ on my left,
Christ in breadth, Christ in length, Christ in height,
Christ in the heart of everyone who thinks of me,
Christ in the mouth of everyone who speaks of me,
Christ in every eye that sees me,
Christ in every ear that hears me.

ATTRIBUTED TO ST. PATRICK

PRAYER OF ST. FRANCIS

Lord, make me an instrument
    of your peace.
Where there is hatred, let me sow love;
    where there is injury, pardon;
    where there is doubt, faith;
    where there is despair, hope;
    where there is darkness, light;
    where there is sadness, joy.
O Divine Master,
Grant that I may not so much seek
    to be consoled, as to console,
    to be understood, as to understand,
    to be loved, as to love.
For it is in giving that we receive;
it is in pardoning that we are pardoned;
it is in dying that we are born to eternal life.

ST. FRANCIS OF ASSISI

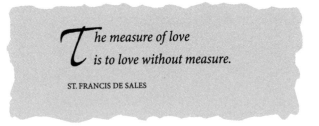

*The measure of love
is to love without measure.*

ST. FRANCIS DE SALES

A PRAYER FOR
COLLEGE STUDENTS

God has created me to do some definite service;
God has committed some work to me
    which has not been committed to another.
I have my mission—I may never know it in this life,
    but I shall be told it in the next.
I am a link in the chain,
    a bond of connection between persons.
God has not created me for naught.
I shall do good.
I shall do God's work.
I shall be an angel of peace,
    a preacher of truth in my own place.
Whatever, wherever I am,
    I can never be thrown away.
If I am in sickness, my sickness may serve the Lord;
    in perplexity, my perplexity may serve the Lord;
        if I am in sorrow, my sorrow may serve the Lord.
God does nothing in vain.
Therefore I will trust in the Lord. Amen.

JOHN HENRY CARDINAL NEWMAN

PRAYER BEFORE STUDY

Creator of all things,
    true source of light and wisdom,
        kindly let a ray of your brilliance
    into the darkness of my understanding.

Grant me a sharp sense
    of understanding,
  a retentive memory,
    and the ability to grasp things correctly.
Grant me the talent of being exact in my explanations
  and the ability to express myself
    with thoroughness and charm.
Point out the beginning,
  direct the progress,
    and help in the completion.
And should I do less well than I would want,
  grant me the insight to see your gift in that. Amen.

BASED ON A PRAYER OF ST. THOMAS AQUINAS

PRAYER FOR LIFE

Father, we praise you for the work of your hands.
For human life, made in your image,
  for the gift of your Son who saved our nature,
  for the power of your Spirit who fills our hearts,
  for all you bestow upon us,
    we praise you, we thank you, we bless you.
Help us to protect the life you gave us:
  support the aged, guide the young,
  lift up the failing, and heal the sick.
To all people grant your truth in its fullness.
May those who are yet unborn soon see the light of day
  and live to give you glory, through Christ our Lord.
Amen.

RESPECT LIFE SUNDAY

ANYWAY

People are often unreasonable,
    illogical, and self-centered;
        forgive them anyway.
If you are kind, people may accuse you
    of selfish, ulterior motives;
        be kind anyway.
If you are successful, you will win some false friends
    and some true enemies;
        succeed anyway.
If you are honest and frank, people may cheat you;
    be honest and frank anyway.
What you spend years building,
    someone could destroy overnight;
        build anyway.
If you find serenity and happiness, they may be jealous;
    be happy anyway.
The good you do today,
    people will often forget tomorrow;
        do good anyway.
Give the world the best you have,
    and it may never be enough;
        give the world the best you've got anyway.
You see, in the final analysis, it is between you and God;
    it was never between you and them, anyway.

BLESSED MOTHER TERESA OF CALCUTTA

FOR MODESTY

Grant unto us, O Lord, the gift of modesty.
When we speak, teach us to give our opinion
    quietly and sincerely.
When we do well in work or play,
    give us a sense of proportion,
        that we be neither unduly elated
    nor foolishly self-deprecatory.
Help us in success to realize what we owe to you
    and to the efforts of others.
In failure, help us to avoid dejection.
And in all ways
    to be simple and natural,
        quiet in manner and lowly in thought.
Through Christ our Lord. Amen.

JOSEPH CARDINAL BERNARDIN

*No ray of sunshine is ever lost,
but the green which it awakes
into existence needs time to sprout, and it
is not always granted to the sower to see the
harvest. All work that is worth anything is
done in faith.*   ALBERT SCHWEITZER

PRAYER FOR PEACE

To you, Creator of nature and humanity, I pray:
Hear my voice, for it is the voice of the victims of all wars
    and violence among individuals and nations.
Hear my voice, for it is the voice of all children who suffer
    and will suffer when people put their faith
        in weapons and war.
Hear my voice, for I speak for the multitudes
    in every country and in every period of history
        who do not want war
    and are ready to walk the road of peace.
Hear my voice and grant insight and strength
    so that we may always respond to hatred with love,
        to injustice with total dedication to justice,
        to need with the sharing of self,
        to war with peace.
O God, hear my voice, and grant unto the world
    your everlasting peace. Amen.

POPE JOHN PAUL II

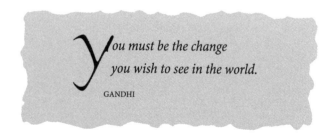

You must be the change you wish to see in the world.

GANDHI

NADA TE TURBE

Nada te turbe.
Nada te espante.
Todo se pasa.
Dios no se muda.
La paciencia todo lo alcanza.
Quien a Dios tiene nada le falta.
Solo Dios basta.

Let nothing disturb you.
Let nothing dismay you.
All things pass.
God never changes.
Patience attains all that is strived for.
He who has God finds he lacks nothing.
God alone suffices.

ST. TERESA OF AVILA

WISDOM

O God,
You created all things according to your plan.
In this very moment,
I know you guide and govern the world.
Grant me the serenity
    to accept the things I cannot change,
        the courage to change the things I can,
    and the wisdom to know the difference.
Living one day at a time,
    enjoying one moment at a time,
        accepting hardships as a pathway to peace,
    taking as Jesus did,
        this sinful world as it is,
    not as I would have it,
        trusting that
    you would make all things right
        if I surrender to your will,
    so that I may be reasonably happy in this life
        and supremely happy with you forever in the next.
I ask this through Christ our Lord. Amen.

REINHOLD NIEBUHR

SLOW ME DOWN, LORD

Slow me down, Lord.
Ease the pounding of my heart
   by the quieting of my mind.
Steady my hurried pace
   with a vision of the eternal reach of time.
Give me, amidst the confusion of my day,
   the calmness of the everlasting hills.
Break the tension of my nerves and muscles
   with the soothing music of singing streams
      that live in my memories.
Help me to know the magical, restorative power
   of your touch.
Teach me the art of taking minute vacations,
   slowing down to look at a flower,
   to chat with a friend,
   to pet a dog.
Remind me each day of the fable of the hare
     and the tortoise
   so that I may know that the race is not always won
    by the swift.
There is more to life than increasing its speed.
Let me look upward into the branches of the towering oak,
   and know that it grew slowly and well.
Slow me down, Lord.
Inspire me to send my roots deep
   into the soil of life's enduring values.

RICHARD CARDINAL CUSHING

PRAYER OF PARADOX AND HUMILITY

I asked God for strength that I might achieve.
I was made weak, that I might learn humbly to obey.

I asked for health, that I might do greater things.
I was given infirmity, that I might do better things.

I asked for riches, that I might be happy.
I was given poverty, that I might be wise.

I asked for things that I might enjoy life.
I was given life, that I might enjoy all things.

I got nothing that I asked for,
    but everything that I had hoped for.
Despite myself, my prayers were answered.
I, among all people, am most richly blessed!

ANONYMOUS CIVIL WAR SOLDIER
Submitted by VERONICA DAVIDSON, *Howard Hall*

PRAYER OF PREPARATION
FOR EUCHARISTIC MINISTERS

Loving God,
Thank you for calling me
    to serve you and your people
        as a minister of the Eucharist.
Help me to be an example of Christian living
    in faith and conduct.

Make me especially mindful
    of your command
  to love my neighbor, remembering that,
    though many, we are one body because
  we share the one bread and cup.
Strengthen my faith and increase my holiness
  that I may always minister with the utmost care
    and reverence for you and your faithful people.
Amen.

PRAYER OF PREPARATION
FOR LECTORS

Everlasting God,
  bless and strengthen me
    as I prepare to proclaim your loving word,
  a word that calls me to respond in faith and love.
Make me a hollow reed,
  so that your voice will be heard
    by all who will hear me.
Free me from any anxiety
  so that with deep faith and confident voice
I may announce your saving word.
May your Spirit fill me
  as it fills the holy word
    that I am about to proclaim.
  Amen.

PRAYER OF PREPARATION
FOR MUSIC MINISTERS

Lord God,
I give thanks for this opportunity
    to use my gift of music in your honor.
Let me be an instrument of prayer and channel
    of your grace.
May the music and song of this sacred worship
      be not a performance
    but my prayer to you,
    my service to the community,
    and my gratitude for the gifts and talents
      that you have bestowed upon me.
I am yours, direct me. Amen.

PRAYER OF ONE WHO FEELS REJECTED

O God, I wasn't counted worthy.
The pain of rejection
    is great enough to be denied.
It's so easy to pretend
    that it doesn't matter.
But the truth is that it hurts
    when others account me of little worth.
Teach me to face the truth.
Teach me to own the hurt
    and not to become calloused
      toward my own feelings
    or those of another.

Teach me to live and to love
    in the midst of this pain.
Teach me to learn and to grow
      in wisdom, word, and deed,
    that your name may be praised
      in all that I am;
    in Christ's name I pray.
Amen.

VIENNA COBB ANDERSON

PRAYER FOR THOSE SUFFERING WITH ILLNESS

Bless, O God, ...
    and all who struggle with illness.
Empower them with hope
    for each and every day.
Provide them with loving and tender care,
    laughter, and the support of love.
Grant them courage when they are afraid,
    comfort when they are in pain,
and your blessing
    when all else seems hopeless,
that in their fight with illness
    they may continue to praise you
and glorify your name;
    in Christ's name we pray. Amen.

VIENNA COBB ANDERSON

FOR INNER HEALING

Holy Spirit,
come and shine the rays of your healing light
    into the depths of my being.
Expose the darkness of my wounds,
    my brokenness and my buried emotions—
        my anger, anxiety, and sorrow.
Give me the courage to acknowledge them,
    to hand them over into your loving care
    and to forgive all those who have hurt me.

Gentle Spirit, I thirst for your healing
    as an arid desert thirsts for rain.
Take the little deaths I have suffered
    and transform them into new life.
Take my pain and transform it
        into the power to serve you with all my strength
    and to proclaim your goodness to others. Amen.

NANCY BENVENGA

*L ord, I do not ask that I never be afflicted,
but only that you never abandon me
in affliction.* ST. BERNADETTE

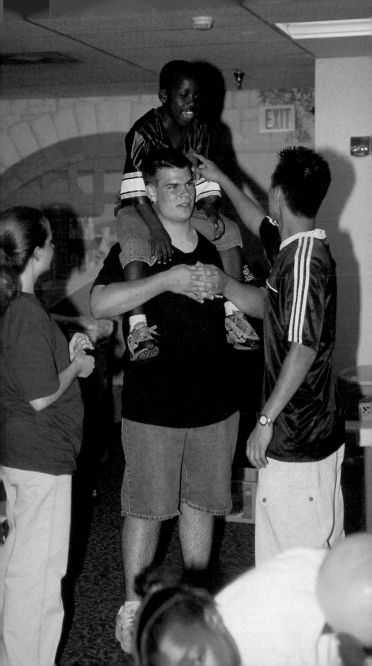

HEALING OF
RELATIONSHIPS

Lord Jesus,
Something is not right
    in my relationship with . . . . .
        and I am hurting.
I cannot lay all the blame on . . . . .
    but neither can I completely
        take the blame myself.
I just know that we need somehow to start over—
    to acknowledge where we have gone wrong,
    to forgive and to forget the past.

Dear Jesus,
    you know the pain of having important
        relationships go wrong,
    and so I am coming to you for help.
Please touch my heart and . . . . .
    with the balm of your healing love.
Help us to set things right
    so that our relationship
        may once again be a source of joy
    and grace for us both. Amen.

NANCY BENVENGA

*God is bread
    when you're hungry,
        water when you're thirsty,
a harbor from the storm.
God's a father to the fatherless,
    a mother to the motherless.
God is my sister, my brother,
    my leader, my guide,
my teacher, my comforter,
        my friend.
God's my all, in all, my everything.*

SISTER THEA BOWMAN

AN INDIAN PRAYER

O Great Spirit,
whose voice I hear in the winds
    and whose breath gives life to all the world, hear me!
I am small and weak,
    I need your strength and wisdom.
Let me walk in beauty, and make my eyes
    ever behold the red and purple sunset.
Make my hands respect the things you have made
    and my ears sharp to hear your voice.
Make me wise so that I may understand
    the things you have taught my people.
Let me learn the lessons you have hidden
    in every leaf and rock.
I seek strength, not to be greater than my brother,
    but to fight my greatest enemy—myself.
Make me always ready to come to you
    with clean hands and straight eyes.
So when life fades, as the fading sunset,
    my spirit will come to you without shame.

RED CLOUD INDIAN SCHOOL,
located on the Pine Ridge Indian Reservation in South Dakota.
For information regarding volunteer opportunities please write:
Red Cloud Indian School; Pine Ridge, SD; 57770
Sumitted by JOHN SAYLOR, *Rolfs Aquatic Center*

WORDS OF OUR LADY OF GUADALUPE TO JUAN DIEGO

Escucha, ponlo en tu corazón, hijo mio el menor,
    que no es nada lo que te espantó, lo que te afligió;
    que no se perturbe tu rostro, tu corazón;
        no temas esta enfermedad
    ni ninguna otra enfermedad, ni cosa punzante,
    aflictiva.
¿No estoy aquí, yo, que soy tu madre?
¿No estás bajo mi sombra y resguardo?
¿No soy yo la fuente de tu alegría?
¿No estás en el hueco de mi manto,
    en el cruce de mis brazos?
¿Tienes necesidad de alguna otra cosa?
 Que ninguna otra cosa te aflija, te perturbe;
    que [nada] te apriete con pena…

Listen, put it in your heart, my son the littlest one,
    that it is nothing that frightened you, that afflicted you;
        that nothing should disturb your face, your heart;
    do not fear this illness nor any other disease,
        nor any harshness or affliction.
Am I not here, I who am your Mother?
Are you not under the shadow of my protection?
Am I not the source of your joy?
Are you not in the hollow of my mantle,
    in the crossing of my arms?
Do you have need of any other thing?
Let no other thing afflict you, disturb you;
    let nothing press you with pain. . .

LITANY OF OUR LADY
OF GUADALUPE

Siempre Virgen Santa María,

Ruega por nosotros.
Holy Mary, ever virgin,
Pray for us.

Madre del único Dios por quien se vive,

Ruega por nosotros.
Mother of the one true God, through whom all things live,
Pray for us.

Madre del Señor del cielo y de la tierra,

Ruega por nosotros.
Mother of the Lord of heaven and earth,
Pray for us.

Preciosa Madre de Dios,

Ruega por nosotros.
Precious Mother of God,
Pray for us.

Neustra piadosa Madre,

Ruega por nosotros.
Our merciful Mother,
Pray for us.

Remedio de miserias, penas y dolores,

Ruega por nosotros.
Remedy of misery, pain and suffering,
Pray for us.

Señora y Niña nuestra,

Ruega por nosotros.

> *Our Lady and dear Little One,*
> *Pray for us.*

OREMOS:

Acuérdate, Señora y Niña nuestra,

> que un día nos dijiste que era nada lo que nos asustaba
>> y afligía, que no se turbara nuestro corazón
> y que no temiéramos esa enfermedad
>> ni alguna otra enfermedad y angustia.

Cuídanos, tú que eres nuestra Madre y estás aquí,

> y guárdanos en tu regazo
>> y bajo tu sombra y resguardo.

LET US PRAY:

Remember, Our Lady and dear Little One,

> *that once you told us that there was nothing to frighten us*
>> *or afflict us, that our hearts should not be troubled*
> *and that we should not fear sickness*
>> *nor any other disease or anxiety.*

Guard us, you who are our Mother and are here,

and keep us in your lap and under the shadow of your protection.

Praying from the Catholic Tradition

Even though we may desire that our prayer be such a spontaneous part of our daily lives that it becomes as natural as breathing, there are times when words fail us. When powerful emotions of joy, sorrow, or fear overtake us or at other times when prayer does not seem to come so naturally, we are fortunate to belong to a faith tradition that includes prayers that have been taught and handed down through many centuries. It can be a source of strength and comfort to unite ourselves with the many people of our faith community who have prayed with these words long before us.

SIGN OF THE CROSS

In the name of the Father,
and of the Son,
and of the Holy Spirit. Amen.

OUR FATHER

Our Father, who art in heaven,
hallowed be thy name;
thy kingdom come;
thy will be done
on earth as it is in heaven.
Give us this day our daily bread;
and forgive us our trespasses
as we forgive those
who trespass against us;
and lead us not into temptation,
but deliver us from evil.
Amen.

HAIL MARY

Hail Mary, full of grace.
The Lord is with you.
Blessed are you among women,
and blessed is the fruit of your womb, Jesus.
Holy Mary, Mother of God,
pray for us sinners,
now and at the hour of our death. Amen.

DOXOLOGY

Glory to the Father, and to the Son,
and to the Holy Spirit,
as it was in the beginning,
is now, and will be forever. Amen.

APOSTLES' CREED

I believe in God,
the Father Almighty,
Creator of heaven and earth.
I believe in Jesus Christ, his only Son, our Lord.
He was conceived by the power of the Holy Spirit
and born of the Virgin Mary.
He suffered under Pontius Pilate,
was crucified, died, and was buried.
He descended to the dead.
On the third day he rose again.
He ascended into heaven,
and is seated at the right hand of the Father.
He will come again to judge the living and the dead.

I believe in the Holy Spirit,
the holy Catholic Church,
the communion of saints,
the forgiveness of sins,
the resurrection of the body,
and the life everlasting. Amen.

NICENE CREED

We believe in one God,
the Father, the Almighty,
maker of heaven and earth,
of all that is seen and unseen.

We believe in one Lord, Jesus Christ,
the only Son of God,
eternally begotten of the Father,
God from God, light from light, true God from true God,
begotten, not made, one in being with the Father.
Through him all things were made.
Who for us and for our salvation
he came down from heaven:

by the power of the Holy Spirit
he was born of the Virgin Mary, and became man.

For our sake he was crucified under Pontius Pilate;
he suffered, died, and was buried.
On the third day he rose again
in fulfillment of the Scriptures;
he ascended into heaven
and is seated at the right hand of the Father.
He will come again in glory
to judge the living and the dead,
and his kingdom will have no end.

We believe in the Holy Spirit, the Lord, the giver of life,
who proceeds from the Father and the Son.

With the Father and the Son
he is worshiped and glorified.
He has spoken through the Prophets.

We believe in one, holy, catholic and apostolic Church.
We acknowledge one baptism for the forgiveness of sins.
We look for the resurrection of the dead,
and the life of the world to come. Amen.

CANTICLE OF MARY
LUKE 1: 46-55

My soul proclaims the greatness of the Lord;
    my spirit rejoices in God my Savior
        for he has looked with favor on his lowly servant.
From this day all generations will call me blessed.
    The Almighty has done great things for me,
        and holy is his Name.
He has mercy on those who fear him
    in every generation.
He has shown the strength of his arm,
    he has scattered the proud in their conceit.
He has cast down the mighty from their thrones,
    and has lifted up the lowly.
He has filled the hungry with good things,
    and the rich he has sent away empty.
He has come to the help of his servant Israel
    for he has remembered his promise of mercy,
    the promise he made to our fathers,
    to Abraham and his children forever.

CANTICLE OF ZECHARIAH
LUKE 1:68–79

Blessed be the Lord, the God of Israel;
    he has come to his people and set them free.
He has raised up for us a mighty savior,
    born of the house of his servant David.
Through his holy prophets he promised of old
    that he would save us from our enemies,
    from the hands of all who hate us.
He promised to show mercy to our fathers
    and to remember his holy covenant.
This was the oath he swore to our father Abraham:
    to set us free from the hands of our enemies,
      free to worship him without fear,
        all the days of our life.
You, my child, shall be called the prophet of the Most High;
    for you will go before the Lord to prepare his way,
      to give his people knowledge of salvation
      by the forgiveness of their sins.
In the tender compassion of our God
    the dawn from on high shall break upon us,
to shine on those who dwell in darkness
    and the shadow of death,
  and to guide our feet into the way of peace.

AN ACT OF FAITH

My God, I place my life in your hands.
I trust you fully, because I know
    you love and care for me.
I believe you are always with me.
I open my mind to your Word
    and my heart to your call.
With the aid of your Holy Spirit,
    help me grow in faith
        as I grow in age and experience.
I ask this in Jesus' name. Amen.

AN ACT OF HOPE

My God, I ground my hope completely in you.
You promised that all things can work together
    for my good, and that absolutely nothing
        can ever separate me from your love.
With you, good overcomes evil,
    joy transforms sorrow, and life conquers death.
Fill me with your Holy Spirit
    so that I may grow in hope
        no matter what evils I face.
I ask this in the name of Jesus Christ, your Son. Amen.

AN ACT OF LOVE

My God, I love you because you are so good,
    and because you love me so much.
I love you in loving myself,
    because your love makes me lovable.
I love you in loving other people,
    because your love gives them life and dignity.
I love you in loving the world,
    because the world reveals your creative presence.
Through the Holy Spirit let my love grow ever deeper.
I ask this in Jesus' name. Amen.

MORNING OFFERING

O Jesus, through the Immaculate Heart of Mary,
I offer you my prayers, works,
    joys, and sufferings of this day,
        in union with the Holy Sacrifice of the Mass
          throughout the world.
I offer them for all the intentions of your Sacred Heart:
    the salvation of souls, reparation for sin,
        the reunion of all Christians. Amen.

AN ACT OF CONTRITION

O my God, I am heartily sorry
        for having offended you,
    and I detest all my sins,
        because of your just punishments,

but most of all because they offend you,
   my God, who are all good
      and deserving of all my love.
I firmly resolve,
   with the help of your grace,
      to sin no more and
   to avoid the near occasions of sin. Amen.

AN ACT OF CONTRITION

O my God,
   I am sincerely sorry for all of my sins.
In choosing to do wrong
   and in failing to do what is right,
I have sinned against you,
   the very source of Love,
      whom I should have before me at all times.
I firmly intend, with your help,
   to be reconciled through my penance,
      to sin no more,
   and to avoid whatever leads me to sin.
Our Savior Jesus Christ suffered and died for us.
In his name, my Lord and God,
   have mercy on me, whom you love. Amen.

MEMORARE

Remember, O most gracious Virgin Mary,
　　　that never was it known
　　that anyone who fled to your protection,
　　implored your help, or sought your intercession
　　　was left unaided.
Inspired by this confidence, we fly unto you,
　　O Virgin of virgins, our Mother!
To you we come, before you we stand,
　　sinful and sorrowful.
O Mother of the Word incarnate,
　　　depise not our petitions,
　　but in your mercy hear and answer us. Amen.

GRACE BEFORE MEALS

Bless us, O Lord, and these your gifts
　　which we are about to receive, from your bounty,
　　　through Christ our Lord. Amen.

GRACE AFTER MEALS

We give you thanks for these
　　and all your gifts, almighty God.
You live and rule forever. Amen.

BLESSING BEFORE MEALS

Lord, the lover of life,
    you feed the birds of the skies
        and array the lilies of the field.
We bless you for all your creatures
    and for the food we are about to receive.
We humbly pray that in your goodness
    you will provide for our brothers and sisters
        who are hungry.
We ask this through Christ our Lord. Amen.

BLESSING AFTER MEALS

Lord, you feed every living thing.
We have eaten together at this table;
    keep us in your love.
Give us true concern
        for the least of our sisters and brothers,
    so that, as we gladly share our food with them,
        we may also sit down together with them
    at the table of the kingdom of heaven.
We ask this through Christ our Lord. Amen.

SUSCIPE
TAKE, LORD, RECEIVE

Take, Lord, and receive all my liberty,
   my memory, my understanding,
      and my entire will,
   all that I have and possess.
You have given all to me; to you, O Lord,
      now I return it; all is yours,
   dispose of me wholly according to your will.
Give me only your love and your grace,
   for this is enough for me.

ST. IGNATIUS OF LOYOLA

PRAYER OF CONSECRATION

O Everlasting and Triune God,
   I consecrate myself wholly to you today.
Let all my days offer you ceaseless praise,
   my hands move to the rhythm
      of your impulses,
   my feet be swift in your service,
   my voice sing constantly of you,
   my lips proclaim your message,
   my eyes perceive you everywhere,
   and my ears be attuned to your inspirations.

May my intellect be filled
    with your wisdom,
  my will be moved by your beauty,
  my heart be enraptured with your love,
  and my soul be flooded with your grace.
Grant that every action of mine be done
    for your greater glory
  and the advancement of my salvation. Amen.

PRAYER AFTER MASS

O Lord Jesus Christ,
  let your passion be my strength
    to sustain, guard, and protect me.
Let your wounds be my food and drink
  to nourish, fill, and invigorate me.
Let the shedding of your blood
  cleanse me of all my sins.
Let your death obtain eternal life for me
  and your cross lead me to everlasting glory.
Let these constitute for me
  refreshment and joy,
    health and uprightness of heart.

ST. PIUS X

COME, HOLY SPIRIT

Come, Holy Spirit, fill the hearts
 of your faithful.
And kindle in them the fire of your love.
Send forth your Spirit and they shall be created.
And you will renew the face of the earth.

O God, who by the light of the Holy Spirit
instructs the hearts of the faithful,
grant, that by the same Holy Spirit we may be truly wise
and ever rejoice in his consolations.
Through Christ our Lord. Amen.

ANIMA CHRISTI
SOUL OF CHRIST

Soul of Christ, sanctify me.
Body of Christ, save me.
Blood of Christ, fill me.
Water flowing from the side of Christ, wash me.
Passion of Christ, strengthen me.

O good Jesus, hear me.
Within your wounds, hide me.
Never permit me to be separated from you.
From the wicked enemy defend me.
At the hour of death call me
 and bid me to come unto you.
That with your saints I may praise you
 forever and ever. Amen.

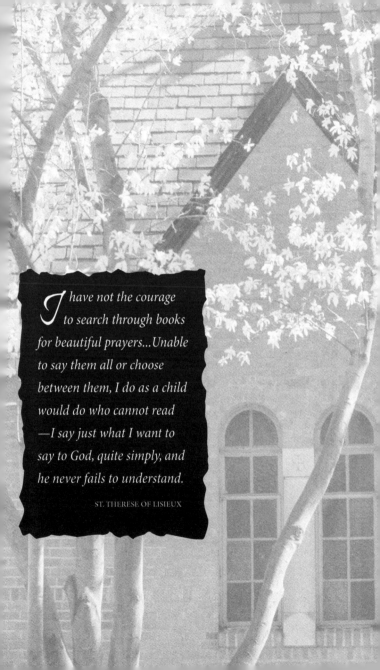

I have not the courage
to search through books
for beautiful prayers...Unable
to say them all or choose
between them, I do as a child
would do who cannot read
—I say just what I want to
say to God, quite simply, and
he never fails to understand.

ST. THERESE OF LISIEUX

Examination of Conscience for Students

FAITH IN GOD

— Do I defend my faith when faced with questions about it?

— Do I stand up for what I believe?

— Do I share my faith with others?

— Do I know enough about my religion to share it effectively with others?

— Do I respect the faith and beliefs of others?

— Am I open to the mystery of God revealed each day to me?

ACTIONS AND DECISIONS

— Do I go along with the crowd, or do I make decisions based on my beliefs and values?

— Can others identify me as a Christian by my speech, actions, and attitudes?

FORGIVENESS

— Do I seek forgiveness?

— Do I forgive?

— Do I hold a grudge?

— Do I have the ability to forgive even the person who doesn't really deserve it?

SUNDAYS...

— Do I come to Mass as a willing
and active participant?

— Do I help build a sense of community?

— Do I appreciate the gift of the Eucharist, and this
opportunity to speak to and to listen to God?

...AND THE REST OF THE WEEK

— Am I aware of God in my life on days other than
Sunday?

— How does God enter into my studies, extra-
curriculars, and relationships?

— What are the top three priorities in my life?
Is God there? If not, then where?

HOSPITALITY

— Do I welcome new students and make them feel
at home?

— Do I reach out to those who may feel lost?

— Do I belong to a clique?

— When was the last time I extended my circle of
friends to include another student?

STUDENT LIFE

— Do I see Jesus in other students?
— Do I follow through on my promises and commitments?
— Do I procrastinate?
— Am I faithful to regular times for study, prayer, exercise?
— Do I thank God each day?
— Do I pray each day for my family, friends, and the concerns of the world?

SELF-AWARENESS

— Am I comfortable with myself and my environment?
— Do I accept what I cannot change?
— Do I have a sense of humor?
— Do I have the ability to laugh at myself?
— Am I hooked on fads? Addicted to drugs? alcohol? tobacco? sex? possessions?
— Do I treat others as objects, especially in sexual ways?
— Do I make sexist remarks?
— Do I try to communicate well with my parents, roommate, and friends?
— Am I truthful and honest in all I say and do?
— Have I done violence to others by damaging their reputation, honor, or material possessions?

REV. GEORGE MATANIC, O.P.

PRAYER OF RECONCILIATION

Come, Holy Spirit,
 enlighten the darkness of my understanding
  and sharpen my conscience,
 so that I may recognize God's will in all things.
Send forth your light and truth into my soul!
May I see all my sins and failures in this light
 and confess them with a contrite heart.
Jesus Christ, gentle Savior,
 I put my hope of salvation in you.
Accept my confession with loving mercy
 and move my heart to true sorrow for my sins.
Heavenly Father,
 when you look into my soul,
  look not so much at the evil I have done,
 but at the genuine sorrow which I feel within my heart.
Help me to confess all my sins
 with a childlike trust in your loving forgiveness. Amen.

The Sacrament of Reconciliation

After an examination of conscience, and in the spirit of sorrow, these steps are followed:

1. The priest greets the penitent.

2. The penitent confesses his or her sins.

3. The priest assists with counsel, and penance is given.

4. An *Act of Contrition* is recited.

5. The priest offers absolution.

Praying the Rosary

The rosary was given to us by a French Dominican, Blessed Alan de la Roche, 1425–1475, who attributed it to St. Dominic. The mysteries of the rosary reflect on significant moments in the lives of Jesus and Mary, events rooted in Scripture.

1. Make the *Sign of the Cross* and pray
   the *Apostles' Creed* on the crucifix.
2. Pray an *Our Father* on the first bead.
3. Pray one *Hail Mary* on each of the next three beads.
4. Pray the *Doxology:* "Glory to the Father…"
5. Announce the mystery for reflection before
   praying the next set of 10 beads, called a decade.
6. Pray an *Our Father* on the single bead.
   Pray a *Hail Mary* on each bead of the decade.
7. Finish the decade with the *Doxology.*
8. Repeat this process (5,6,7) for each decade.
9. At the end of the last decade,
   pray the *Hail Holy Queen.*

At the end of each decade,
many add the Fatima Invocation:
O my Jesus, forgive us our sins,
save us from the fires of hell, and lead all souls to heaven,
especially those most in need of thy mercy.

THE MYSTERIES
OF THE ROSARY

JOYFUL MYSTERIES *(Mondays and Saturdays)*

1. The Annunciation of the Birth of the Lord to Mary
   (Luke 1:26–38)
2. The Visitation of Mary to her Cousin Elizabeth
   (Luke 1:39–56)
3. The Nativity of our Lord Jesus Christ
   (Matthew 1: 18–25; Luke 2:1–20)
4. The Presentation of the Infant Jesus in the Temple
   (Luke 2:22–38)
5. The Finding of the Child Jesus in the Temple
   (Luke 2:41–52)

SORROWFUL MYSTERIES *(Tuesdays and Fridays)*

1. The Agony in the Garden of Gethsemane
   (Mark 14:32–42)
2. The Scourging of Jesus at the Pillar
   (John 18:28–38; 19:1)
3. The Crowning with Thorns *(Mark 15:16–20)*
4. The Carrying of the Cross *(John 19: 12–17)*
5. The Crucifixion and Death of Jesus
   (Mt. 27: 33–56; Mk.15: 22–41; Luke 23:26–49; Jn.19:16–30)

LUMINOUS MYSTERIES *(Thursdays)*

1. The Baptism of Jesus in the Jordan *(Matthew 3:13–17)*
2. The Wedding Feast of Cana *(John 2:1–12)*
3. The Proclamation of the Kingdom of God
   (Mark 1:15; 2:3–13)
4. The Transfiguration of Jesus *(Matthew 17: 1–8; Luke 9:28–36)*
5. The First Eucharist *(Matthew 26:26–30)*

GLORIOUS MYSTERIES *(Wednesdays and Sundays)*

1. The Resurrection of Jesus *(Luke 24:1–12; John 20)*
2. The Ascension of Jesus into Heaven
   (Luke 24:50–53; Acts 2: 1–4)
3. The Coming of the Holy Spirit *(Acts 2:1–4)*
4. The Assumption of Mary into Heaven *(Song of Songs 2:8–14)*
5. The Coronation of Mary *(Revelation 12:1–6)*

HAIL, HOLY QUEEN
(concluding the rosary)

Hail, holy Queen, Mother of Mercy,
    our life, our sweetness, and our hope.
To you do we cry, poor banished children of Eve.
To you do we send up our sighs,
    mourning and weeping in this valley of tears.
Turn, then, most gracious advocate,
    your eyes of mercy toward us,
        and after this, our exile,
    show unto us the blessed fruit of your womb, Jesus.
O clement, O loving, O sweet Virgin Mary.
Pray for us, O holy Mother of God,
    that we may be made worthy of the promises of Christ.

THE ANGELUS

*The Angelus is traditionally prayed in the
early morning, at noon, and in the evening. The faithful stop
their work to pray. In many places they are called to pray the
Angelus at the pealing of the church bells at 6 a.m., noon, and
6 p.m.*

The angel of the Lord declared unto Mary,
and she conceived by the Holy Spirit.

Hail, Mary…

Behold the handmaid of the Lord.
Be it done unto me according to your word.

Hail, Mary…

And the Word was made flesh,
and dwelt among us.

Hail, Mary…

Pray for us, O holy Mother of God,
that we may be made worthy of the promises of Christ.

Pour forth, we beseech you, O Lord,
    your grace into our hearts,
that we, to whom the incarnation of Christ, your Son,
    was made known by the message of an angel,
        may by his passion and cross
    be brought to the glory of his resurrection,
        through the same Christ our Lord. Amen.

QUEEN OF HEAVEN
REGINA COELI

This Easter antiphon is used during the Easter season
instead of the usual Angelus prayers.

O Queen of Heaven, rejoice, alleluia,
for the Son whom you were privileged to bear, alleluia,
has risen as he said, alleluia.
Pray for us to God, alleluia.
Rejoice and be glad, O Virgin Mary, alleluia.
for the Lord has truly risen, alleluia.

O God, you gave joy to the world
through the Resurrection of your Son,
our Lord Jesus Christ.
Grant that we may obtain,
through his Virgin Mother, Mary,
the joys of everlasting life
through the same Christ our Lord. Amen.

Work as though all depends on you.
Pray as though all depends on God.

ST. IGNATIUS OF LOYOLA

Praying before the Blessed Sacrament

Adoration of the Blessed Sacrament is an ancient prayer of the Church which continues to be done in private and in common. Adoration can be done in any chapel or church where the Blessed Sacrament is reserved (kept in the tabernacle) or exposed (a consecrated host is taken from the tabernacle and placed in a monstrance which "exposes" the host for all to see). Pope John Paul II wrote in his Letter on the 750th Anniversary of the Feast of Corpus Christi that "Remaining in silence before the Blessed Sacrament, it is Christ totally and really present whom we discover, whom we adore, and with whom we are in contact."

Prayer before the Blessed Sacrament is one way to nourish our spiritual lives. There are many books, devotional prayers, hymns, and songs that may accompany or be part of adoration—these are not ends in themselves but guides to deeper communion with God. Spending silent time before the Blessed Sacrament to speak with Jesus and to listen to him should lead us to act more like Christ in our lives and build his Kingdom on earth.

TO PRAY BEFORE THE BLESSED SACRAMENT

— *Find a church or chapel where the Blessed Sacrament is reserved or exposed.*
— *Upon entering the chapel, make a sign of reverence (genuflect) and find a seat or kneeler where it is possible to pray in the presence of the Blessed Sacrament.*
— *Use scripture, meditation books, devotional prayers, etc. Pray from your heart. Remember that Jesus is our friend;*

speak to him as you would a friend (tell him what's going on—both joys and sorrows, what's causing anxieties, what graces you would like him to give, etc…) and remember to leave time to listen.)

Below is a common prayer form that is used for adoration. Pray slowly and listen to Jesus' words of response.

I. OPENING PRAYER

I have come, my Lord, to be with you, to recall the great mystery of faith: your true presence in the consecrated bread of life. I come to adore you, Jesus, by acts of faith, hope, and love. I wish to express sorrow for my sins, to make reparation for the sins of the whole world, to thank you for your blessings and gifts, and to present to you my needs, my fears, and my desire for you to govern my life.

I pray to the Holy Spirit of light and truth to fill my heart and enkindle the fire of your divine love. I also ask our Blessed Mother to be with me as I visit her Divine Son.

Lord, I may not be able to find all the words to express what is really in my heart. I may be distracted and perhaps feel weariness. Regardless, I kneel in silence before you, knowing that you know my innermost thoughts and desires.

I come to renew my personal love for you, and to attempt to rededicate my life to you. Please touch my heart and my soul with your peace. Amen.

II. PRAYER BEFORE
THE BLESSED SACRAMENT

Eucharistic Heart of Jesus, fill my heart with that same love that burned in your heart. May I become love and mercy to those who live in pain and suffering. May I become the living gospel of your compassionate love.

Eucharistic Heart of Jesus, fill me with faith, hope, and love. When I find myself lacking in charity, help me to see your presence in those around me. Increase my faith when I find it hard to understand. Give me hope when life around me seems empty and forsaken. May your presence in the Blessed Sacrament of the altar be my courage and strength.

Eucharistic Heart of Jesus, your gift of the holy Eucharist strengthens me on the journey of life. Transform me into your disciple and send me to those who are in need of your love. May I be your hands to those who are helpless. May I be your heart to those who are unloved. Surround me with your light and allow me to be an instrument of your peace.

Eucharistic Heart of Jesus, many times I find life to be difficult and filled with anxiety. Help me in times of uncertainty to come into your Eucharistic presence. Be my strength, my rock, my fortress, and my refuge. Help me, by the power of your Holy Spirit, to feel the light of your Resurrection surrounding me and protecting me from all danger. In you I hope, Lord; may I never be disappointed. Amen.

III. ACT OF SPIRITUAL COMMUNION

Lord Jesus Christ, I believe that you are present body, blood, soul, and divinity in the sacrament of the Eucharist. I love you and desire you. Come into my heart. I embrace you. Never let me be parted from your love. Amen.

IV. DIVINE PRAISES

Blessed be God.
Blessed be his holy name.
Blessed be Jesus Christ, true God and true man.
Blessed be the name of Jesus.
Blessed be his most Sacred Heart.
Blessed be his most Precious Blood.
Blessed be Jesus in the most Holy Sacrament of the Altar.
Blessed be the Holy Spirit, the Paraclete.
Blessed be the great mother of God, Mary, most holy.
Blessed be her holy and Immaculate Conception.
Blessed be her glorious Assumption.
Blessed be the name of Mary, Virgin and Mother.
Blessed be Saint Joseph, her most chaste spouse.
Blessed be God in his angels and in his saints.

V. CLOSING PRAYER

Lord God, Father of mercy and source
of life, you call us from the whole world to celebrate
with renewed fervor the great mystery of the Eucharist,
memorial for all time of the Passover of your Son.

With gratitude in our hearts from the salvation, which
has been given us, we ask you confidently: make us one
body in Christ. May we live the divine life, which he
obtained for us at the price of his Blood.

Enlivened by his Holy Spirit, we will proclaim to the
world the wonders of your love.

We make this prayer through Jesus Christ your Son, who
was born of the Virgin and who lives and reigns with you
in the unity of the Holy Spirit, one God forever and ever.
Amen.

I still believe that standing up for the truth of God is the greatest thing in the world. This is the end of life. The end of life is not to be happy.

The end of life is not to achieve pleasure and avoid pain.

The end of life is to do the will of God, come what may.

REV. MARTIN LUTHER KING JR.

KNOWING THE CATHOLIC FAITH

THE SEVEN SACRAMENTS

SACRAMENTS OF INITIATION
Baptism
Confirmation
Holy Eucharist

SACRAMENTS OF HEALING
Reconciliation
Anointing of the Sick

SACRAMENTS OF VOCATION
Holy Orders
Matrimony

THE TWO GREAT COMMANDMENTS
Matthew 22:36–38

When asked which commandment is the greatest,
this was Jesus' answer:
"You shall love the Lord your God with all your
heart, and with all your soul, and with all your mind.
You shall love your neighbor as yourself."

157

THE TEN COMMANDMENTS
Exodus 20:1–17 and Deuteronomy 5:6–22

1. I, the Lord, am your God.
   You shall not have other gods besides me.
2. You shall not take the name
   of the Lord, your God, in vain.
3. Remember to keep holy the Sabbath day.
4. Honor your father and your mother.
5. You shall not kill.
6. You shall not commit adultery.
7. You shall not steal.
8. You shall not bear false witness against your
   neighbor.
9. You shall not covet your neighbor's wife.
10. You shall not covet your neighbor's goods.

THE BEATITUDES
Matthew 5:3–10

Blessed are the poor in spirit,
   for theirs is the kingdom of heaven.
Blessed are they who mourn,
   for they will be comforted.
Blessed are the meek, for they will inherit the land.
Blessed are they who hunger and thirst for
   righteousness, for they will be satisfied.

Blessed are the merciful,
    for they will be shown mercy.
Blessed are the clean of heart, for they will see God.
Blessed are the peacemakers,
    for they will be called children of God.
Blessed are they who are persecuted
    for the sake of righteousness,
    for theirs is the kingdom of heaven.

CORPORAL WORKS OF MERCY

Feed the hungry.
Give drink to the thirsty.
Clothe the naked.
Visit the imprisoned.
Shelter the homeless.
Visit the sick.
Bury the dead.

THE SPIRITUAL WORKS
OF MERCY

Admonish the sinner.
Instruct the ignorant.
Counsel the doubtful.
Comfort the sorrowful.
Bear wrongs patiently.
Forgive all injuries.
Pray for the living and the dead.

GIFTS OF THE HOLY SPIRIT

Wisdom
Knowledge
Understanding
Piety
Counsel
Fear of the Lord
Fortitude

PRECEPTS OF THE CHURCH

These are intended to be the minimum Catholics should do in the spirit of prayer and moral effort.

Participate in Mass on Sundays and
    Holy Days of Obligation
Confess serious sins at least once a year
Receive Holy Communion at least during
    the Easter Season
Observe the prescribed days of fasting and abstinence
Provide for the material needs of the church,
    according to one's abilities

Praying
Through the Seasons

ADVENT • CHRISTMAS • LENT • EASTER

There is something deep within us that resonates to the changing sights and sounds and the unique traditions and customs that mark our seasonal calendars. The ebb and flow of human life find inspiration and direction in the holy days and holidays that mark the passage of time.

The church sets aside major seasons of the liturgical year, Advent, Christmas, Lent, and Easter, to highlight the primary events and beliefs of our faith. We are invited and challenged to enter into the ongoing mysteries of incarnation, saving birth, conversion, repentance, life, death, and resurrection. During these times of the year, we give our attention to very specific aspects of what God has done and continues to do for and among us.

This section of the book is designed to help you enter more fully into the spirit of these seasons.

ADVENT:WEEK I
WAIT FOR THE LORD

God of Wonder,
our hearts desire the warmth of your love,
     and our minds are searching
   for the light of your Word.
Wake us up to the new morning
   that is waiting for us.
Increase our longing for Christ our Savior,
   and give us the strength to grow in love,
that the dawn of his coming
   will find us rejoicing in his presence
     and welcoming the light of his truth.
We ask this in the name of Jesus the Lord.

ROMANS 13: 11-14

Brothers and sisters:
you know the time;
   it is the hour now for you to awake from sleep.
For our salvation is nearer now
   than when we first believed;
   the night is advanced, the day is at hand.

Let us then throw off the works
     of darkness
   and put on the armor of light;
let us conduct ourselves properly as in the day,
     not in orgies and drunkenness,
     not in promiscuity and lust,
     not in rivalry and jealousy.
But put on the Lord Jesus Christ,
     and make no provision for the desires of the flesh.

ANTIPHON

O Rising Dawn,
   Radiance of the Light Eternal,
Son of Justice, come and enlighten us
   who sit in darkness and in the shadow of death.

✠ O Rising Dawn,
you dispel the darkness and gloom in our lives
     and cast light on our thoughts and concerns.
   Enlighten our minds and hearts
     that we might live in your light
   and begin to recognize your coming
     in one another. Amen.

ADVENT: WEEK II
TEACH US WISDOM

God of Glory and Wisdom,
the day draws near
    when the glory of your Son
  will make radiant the night of our waiting world.
Do not let the obstacle of selfishness
    keep us from the joy
  that is at the end of our Advent path.
May the darkness not blind us to the vision of wisdom
  which fills the minds of those who find him.
Help us, Source of All Kindness,
  to clear out all those things that block our paths.
Let us straighten our crooked ways,
  pull down our distrustful mountains,
    and fill up our valleys of fear.
We ask this in the name of Jesus the Lord.

ISAIAH 2: 2-4

In days to come,
the mountain of the Lord's house
  shall be established as the highest mountain
  and raised above the hills.
All nations shall stream to it;
  many peoples shall come and say:
"Come, let us climb the Lord's mountain,
  to the house of the God of Jacob,

that he may instruct us in his ways,
   and we may walk in his paths."
For from Zion shall go forth instruction,
   and the word of the Lord from Jerusalem.
He shall judge between the nations,
   and impose terms on many peoples.
They shall beat their swords into plowshares
   and their spears into pruning hooks;
one nation shall not raise the sword against another,
   nor shall they train for war again.

ANTIPHON

O Wisdom, O Holy Word of God, you guide all creation
   with your strong yet tender care.
Come to teach us your ways of gentleness and love.

✠ O Wisdom of God,
you have blessed us with the lives of family and friends
   and with the wonders of your creation.
Give us the courage and wisdom
      to be faithful to your Word
   and to follow your example of gentleness and love.
Help us to live in peace and harmony,
   and to share the signs of your coming
      with one another. Amen.

ADVENT: WEEK III
JOY AND HOPE IN THE COMING LORD

God of all our joy,
you are always faithful to your promises
    and always close to your people.
The earth rejoices in the hope
      of the Savior's coming
    and looks forward with longing
      to his return at the end of time.

Prepare our hearts and remove the sadness
    or blindness that hinders us
      from recognizing Jesus,
    and from feeling the joy and hope
      which his presence will bestow,
    for he is Lord forever and ever.

ISAIAH 35:1-6A

The desert and the parched land will exult;
    the steppe will rejoice and bloom.
They will bloom with abundant flowers,
    and rejoice with joyful song.
The glory of Lebanon will be given to them,
    the splendor of Carmel and Sharon;
they will see the glory of the Lord,
    the splendor of our God.

Strengthen the hands that are feeble,
   make firm the knees that are weak,
say to those whose hearts are frightened:
   "Be strong, fear not!
Here is your God,
   he comes with vindication;
with divine recompense
   he comes to save you."
Then will the eyes of the blind be opened,
   the ears of the deaf be cleared;
then will the lame leap like a stag,
   then the tongue of the mute will sing.

ANTIPHON

O Emmanuel, King and Lawgiver,
   Awaited Savior of all Peoples,
come dwell within and set us free,
   O Lord our God.

✠ O Emmanuel,
your name brings us joy
   and our God draws near to us in you.
As we wait in hope for the day of your coming,
      let us recognize your nearness to us
   in the people and events
      of today and every day. Amen.

ADVENT:WEEK IV
OPENNESS TO THE SPIRIT OF GOD

God of gifts and challenges,
  your eternal Word took flesh on our earth
when the Virgin Mary placed her life
  at the service of your plan.

Lift our minds in watchful hope
  to hear the voice which announces his glory
and open our minds to receive the Spirit
  who prepares us for his coming.

Cast out the fear from our hearts.
Let us help others to cast aside their fears
  as the moment of Christmas approaches.

We ask this through Christ our Lord.

LUKE 1:39–45

Mary set out and traveled to the hill country
  in haste to a town of Judah,
    where she entered the house of Zechariah
    and greeted Elizabeth.
When Elizabeth heard Mary's greeting,
  the infant leaped in her womb,
    and Elizabeth, filled with the Holy Spirit,
    cried out in a loud voice and said,

"Blessed are you among women,
    and blessed is the fruit of your womb.
And how does this happen to me,
    that the mother of my Lord should come to me?
For at the moment the sound of your greeting
    reached my ears,
    the infant in my womb leaped for joy.
Blessed are you who believed
    that what was spoken to you by the Lord
    would be fulfilled."

ANTIPHON

O Root of Jesse, Standard to all Peoples,
    the most powerful are silenced in your presence
        and all nations appeal to you.
Come save us, and do not delay!

✠ O Root of Jesse,
you are the greatest sign of God's love for us
    and the fulfillment of the hopes of all people.
Continue to be our source of all goodness
    and help us to be signs of your love
        and grace to one another. Amen.

ADVENT
CHRISTMAS TIME

BLESSING OF THE ADVENT WREATH

By day and by night,
    and through the circle of the seasons,
you keep watch over us, God Most High.
We praise you for this Advent wreath.
It is the evergreen crown of your royal people.
Soon it will grow bright and scatter the darkness.
Around this shining wreath we shall keep watch
        for your Son, our Lord Jesus Christ,
    who comes to comfort our fears
        and to make new this waiting world.
All glory be yours, both now and forever. Amen.

NEW BETHLEHEM

Again the bright entreating star rebukes
The barren welcome that He came to find
For crowded inn, the heart obsessed by pain,
For stable now, the dark and arrogant mind.

And yet with steadfast joy, foreknowing all
Our long despairs made golden in her son,
Into the mourning city of the soul
Mary expectant brings its promised one.

God speed your hour,
    Mother of our Hope!
And even in the citadel of pain
Let us behold him—so our doom shall pass
And the great star shall tell of peace again.

SISTER JEREMY FINNEGAN

BLESSING OF THE TREE

God of Adam and Eve, God of all our ancestors,
    we praise you for this Christmas tree.
It stirs in us a memory of paradise,
    and it brings us a glimpse of heaven.
Send your son Jesus,
       the shoot sprung from the root of Jesse,
    to restore your good earth to the freshness of Eden.
On the day of his coming,
       every tree of the forest will clap its hands in joy,
    and all creation will bless you
       from the shining branches:
Glory in heaven and peace on earth,
    both now and forever. Amen.

BLESSING OF THE CRECHE

Bless us, Lord, as we come to Bethlehem,
    where animals and angels, shepherds and seekers
        together behold your face.
Here snow becomes straw and frost becomes flowers
    as winter melts into everlasting spring.
In our holy Christmas, in this festival of Christ,
    give us the riches of poverty and the power of weakness
as we join the angels in proclaiming your praise:

Glory in heaven and peace on earth,
    now and forever. Amen.

CHRISTMAS PRAYER

Lord,
your only Son embraced the weakness of flesh,
    that we might have power to become your children;
        your eternal Word chose a dwelling among us,
    that we might live in your presence.
With grace upon grace, reveal in our lives
        the share of his fullness we have all received;
    and let us see the glory
        which he has with you and the Holy Spirit
    as God, forever and ever. Amen.

FEAST OF THE HOLY FAMILY

God our Father, we come into your house
    filled with wonder at the extravagance of your love.
You sent your eternal Word among us—
        one like us, yet our Redeemer,
        the only-begotten Son, yet humble in obedience.
Teach us to ponder the mystery of Nazareth
        that we may always find in you
        the source of our strength and the unity of our families.
We ask this through Jesus Christ,
    your Word made flesh. Amen.

MARY, MOTHER OF GOD

Creator God,
you come near to us this Christmas season
    in a child born of the Virgin Mary.
In the depths of darkness, she gave birth to light;
    in the depths of silence, she brought forth the Word.
Grant that we who ponder these things
    in our hearts may recognize in her child
        our Lord and Savior, Jesus Christ,
who reigns with you in the unity of the Holy Spirit,
    in the splendor of eternal light. Amen.

BLESSING OF THE NEW YEAR

God of time and of eternity, God of every generation,
    with Christmas joy we praise you for the year gone by
        and for the year we have begun.
Your Son comes among us
        to bring glad tidings to the poor,
    to proclaim a year acceptable in your sight.
Knit us in harmony and love,
    we who are flesh of his flesh.
Fill the year with good gifts for all the world
    as we join the angels in proclaiming your praise:
Glory in heaven and peace on earth
        now and forever. Amen.

EPIPHANY

Lord of nations,
    we have seen the star of your glory
        rising in splendor.
The radiance of your incarnate Word
    pierces the darkness that covers the earth
        and signals the dawn of peace and justice.
Make radiant the lives of your people
        with that same brightness
    and beckon all the nations
        to walk as one in your light. Amen.

*C*hanged by the working of grace into new creatures, Christians humbly set themselves to follow Christ and learn more and more within the church to think like him, to judge like him, to act in conformity with his commandments, and to hope as he invites us to.

POPE JOHN PAUL II

LENT: ASH WEDNESDAY AND WEEK I

FOR THE SPIRIT OF REPENTANCE

Lord our God,
you formed us from the clay of the earth,
   and breathed into us the spirit of life,
      but we turned from your face and sinned.
Through our observance of Lent,
   help us to understand the meaning
      of your Son's death and resurrection,
   and teach us to reflect it in our lives.
In this time of repentance
   we call out for your mercy.
Bring us back to you
   and to the life your Son won for us
      by his death on the cross,
   for he lives and reigns forever and ever.
Amen.

ROMANS 8:8-11

Brothers and sisters:
those who are in the flesh cannot please God.
But you are not in the flesh;
   on the contrary, you are in the spirit,
   if only the Spirit of God dwells in you.

Whoever does not have the Spirit of
    Christ does not belong to him.
But if Christ is in you,
    although the body is dead because of sin,
    the spirit is alive because of righteousness.
If the Spirit of the one who raised Jesus from the dead
    dwells in you,
the one who raised Christ from the dead
    will give life to your mortal bodies also,
    through his Spirit dwelling in you.

✠ Merciful God,
you call us forth from the dust of the earth;
    you claimed us for Christ in the waters of baptism.
Look upon us as we enter these 40 days
    bearing the mark of ashes, and bless our journey
        through the desert of Lent to the font of rebirth.
May our fasting be hunger for justice;
    our alms, a making of peace;
    our prayer, the chant of humble and graceful hearts.
All that we do and pray is in the name of Jesus,
    for in his cross you proclaim your love
        forever and ever. Amen.

LENT: WEEK II
THE GRACE TO RESPOND TO THE WORD OF GOD

God of Light,
in you is found no shadow of change
    but only the fullness of life and limitless truth.
Open our hearts to the voice of your Word
    and free us from the original darkness
        that shadows our vision.
Restore our sight that we may look upon your Son
    who calls us to repentance and a change of heart,
        for he lives and reigns with you
            forever and ever. Amen.

2 TIMOTHY: 1: 8–10

Beloved:
bear your share of hardship for the gospel
    with the strength that comes from God.
He saved us and called us to a holy life,
    not according to our works
    but according to his own design
    and the grace bestowed on us in Christ Jesus
    before time began,

but now made manifest
   through the appearance of
   our savior Christ Jesus,
who destroyed death and brought life and immortality
   to light through the gospel.

✠ Lord,
you invite us to know you better
   and to follow you.
Enlighten us with your holy Word
   that we may be strengthened
      by your wisdom and truth.
Give us the courage and commitment
      to live according to your precepts,
   and the grace to respond each time
      we are invited to follow you. Amen.

LENT:WEEK III
FORM A NEW HEART WITHIN US

God of all compassion and goodness,
to heal the wounds our sins and
   selfishness bring upon us
you bid us turn to fasting, prayer, and
   sharing with our brothers and sisters.
We acknowledge our sinfulness,
   our guilt is ever before us.
When our weakness causes discouragement,
   let our compassion fill us with hope
and lead us through a Lent of repentance
   to the beauty of Easter joy.
Grant this through Christ our Lord.

EPHESIANS 5: 8-14

Brothers and sisters:
you were once darkness,
   but now you are light in the Lord.
Live as children of light,
   for light produces every kind of goodness
   and righteousness and truth.
Try to learn what is pleasing to the Lord.

Take no part in the fruitless works
of darkness; rather expose them,
for it is shameful even to mention
the things done by them in secret;
but everything exposed by the light becomes visible,
for everything that becomes visible is light.
Therefore, it says:
"Awake, O sleeper,
and arise from the dead,
and Christ will give you light."

✠ Lord of Life,
each day we are confronted with choices
that can bring either darkness or light
to a waiting world.
Help us to be children of the light,
choosing to transform despair and suffering
into life and hope.
Lead us from the darkness of sin
to the light of your love. Amen.

LENT: WEEK IV

BRINGING CHRIST'S PEACE TO OUR WORLD

God of Peace,
your Word, Jesus Christ, spoke peace
    to a sinful world
and brought humankind
    the gift of reconciliation
        by the suffering and death he endured.
Teach us, the people who bear his name,
    to follow the example he gave us.
May our faith, hope, and charity
    turn hatred to love, conflict to peace,
        death to eternal life.
We ask this through Christ our Lord.

2 CORINTHIANS 5:17–21

Brothers and sisters:
    whoever is in Christ is a new creation:
        the old things have passed away;
    behold, new things have come.
And all this is from God,
    who has reconciled us to himself through Christ
        and given us the ministry of reconciliation;
    namely, God was reconciling the world
        to himself in Christ,

not counting their trespasses
    against them
and entrusting to us the message of reconciliation.
So we are ambassadors for Christ,
    as if God were appealing through us.
We implore you on behalf of Christ,
    be reconciled to God.
For our sake he made him to be sin
        who did not know sin,
    so that we might become
        the righteousness of God in him.

✠ Lord,
renew and keep us in your love.
You know our weaknesses well
    and yet you call us to be peacemakers in this world.
Help us to be signs of your love and grace
        in even the smallest parts of everyday life,
    and always mindful
        of how our words and actions affect others. Amen.

LENT : WEEK V
THE COURAGE TO FOLLOW CHRIST

God of all,
the love of your Son led him to accept
    the suffering of the cross
        that we might glory in new life.
Help us to be like Christ your Son,
    who loved the world and died for
        our salvation.
Inspire us by his love,
    guide us by his example.
Change our selfishness into self-giving.
Help us to embrace the world you have given us,
    that we may transform the darkness of its pain
        into the life and joy of Easter. Amen.

ISAIAH 50: 4–7

The Lord God has given me
    a well-trained tongue,
that I might know how to speak to the weary
    a word that will rouse them.
Morning after morning
    he opens my ear that I may hear;
and I have not rebelled,
    have not turned back.

I gave my back to those who beat me,
    my cheeks to those who
    plucked my beard;
my face I did not shield
    from buffets and spitting.
The Lord God is my help,
    therefore I am not disgraced;
I have set my face like flint,
    knowing that I shall not be put to shame.

✠ Lord,
during these days of Lent, give us the courage
    to abandon what is familiar and comfortable
  so that we can take risks
    that will promote growth and change.
Help us to remember your words and example
  so that we will be inspired
    to live the demands of the Gospel.
Give us the strength to walk the Christian path,
    and to see all things
    through the eyes of your endless love. Amen.

LENT: WEEK VI
HOLY WEEK

Holy Week recalls the passion, death, and resurrection of Jesus. Follow the journey to Calvary by praying the Stations of the Cross in the basilica, around the lake, and at other times and places on campus.

THE STATIONS OF THE CROSS

(or the Way of the Cross) consist of an ancient devotion brought back from the Holy Land where pilgrims traced the footsteps of Christ, especially on the Via Dolorosa, the road to Calvary.

Each station usually begins with the versicle and response:
V. We adore you, O Christ, and we praise you.
R. Because by your holy cross you have redeemed the world.

At each station, a meditation is made and a prayer may be added. In public devotions, a verse of the Stabat Mater *is often said or sung after each station. The traditional stations are:*

THE FIRST STATION: **Jesus is condemned to death.**
Mt. 27:26; Mk. 15:15; Lk. 23:24–25; Jn. 19:1

THE SECOND STATION: **Jesus is made to carry the Cross.**
Jn. 19:16

THE THIRD STATION: **Jesus falls the first time.**
Mt. 27:31

THE FOURTH STATION: **Jesus meets his Blessed Mother.** *Jn. 19:25–27*

THE FIFTH STATION:

Simon helps Jesus to carry his cross.
Mk. 15:21

THE SIXTH STATION: **Veronica wipes the face of Jesus.**
Lk. 23:27

THE SEVENTH STATION: **Jesus falls the second time.**
Lk. 23:26

THE EIGHTH STATION: **Jesus speaks to
the women of Jerusalem.** *Lk. 23:28–31*

THE NINTH STATION: **Jesus falls the third time.**
Jn. 19:17

THE TENTH STATION: **Jesus is stripped of
his garments.** *Lk 23:32*

THE ELEVENTH STATION: **Jesus is nailed to the cross.**
Mt. 27:33–38; Mk. 15:22–27; Lk. 23:33–34; Jn. 19:18

THE TWELFTH STATION: **Jesus dies on the cross.**
Mt. 27:46–50; Mk. 15:34–37; Lk. 23:46; Jn. 19:28–30

THE THIRTEENTH STATION: **Jesus is taken down
from the Cross.** *Mt. 27:57–58; Mk. 15:42–45; Lk. 23:50–52; Jn. 19:38*

THE FOURTEENTH STATION: **Jesus is placed
in the tomb.** *Mt. 27:59–61; Mk. 15:46–47; Lk. 23:53–56; Jn. 19:39–42*

THE FIFTEENTH STATION (optional): **The Resurrection.**
Mt. 28; Mk. 16; Lk. 24: Jn. 20

*The stations are usually conducted with prayers for the intentions
of the Holy Father, e.g., an Our Father, a Hail Mary, and the
Doxology. It should be noted that the three falls of Christ and the
meeting between Jesus and Mary on the* Via Dolorosa *are a*

spiritual conclusion of many writers, and there is no historical proof of a St. Veronica. Rather, in her we express the longing that we could have been there and performed this act of compassion.

THE STABAT MATER
SORROWFUL MOTHER

At the cross her station keeping
stood the mournful mother weeping,
close to Jesus to the last.

Through her heart his sorrow sharing,
all his bitter anguish bearing,
lo! the piercing sword had passed.

For his people's sins rejected,
saw her Jesus unprotected,
saw with thorns, with scourges rent.

Saw her son from judgement taken,
her beloved in death forsaken,
till his spirit forth he sent.

Jesus, may your cross defend me,
and your mother's prayers befriend me.
Let me die in your embrace.

When to dust my dust returns,
grant a soul which for you yearns,
in your paradise a place. Amen.

THE PASCHAL TRIDUUM

The Paschal Triduum, meaning "the three days of passover,"
takes place from Holy Thursday sundown to Easter Sunday
sundown and is the heart of the year—the three days of the
death, burial, and resurrection of the Lord. During these holiest
of days, we fast and feast as we celebrate our passover in Christ
on Holy Thursday evening, Good Friday, Holy Saturday, and
Easter Sunday.

Make an effort to attend Holy Week services and let your
prayer these days unite you with the church community in a
spirit of transformation and renewal.

✠ On this most holy night when our Lord, Jesus Christ,
     passed from death to life,
  the church invites her children throughout the world
  to come together in vigil and in prayer.
This is the passover of the Lord.
If we honor the memory of his death and resurrection
  by hearing his Word
    and celebrating his mysteries,
  then we may be confident that we shall share
    his victory over death
  and live with him forever in God.

EASTER VIGIL LITURGY

EASTER

PRAYER FOR EASTER DAY

Fill your church, O God of glory,
   with the power flowing
      from Christ's resurrection,
that we may be present
   in the midst of the world your Son redeemed
as the beginnings
   of a renewed humanity
      risen to new life with Christ. Amen.

PRAYER FOR THE EASTER SEASON

God of life,
   ground of our faith,
with Jesus you have raised us up
   in the waters of baptism
      and given us life that endures.
Day by day refine our faith,
      and remove every trace of unbelief,
   that we may confess Jesus
      as our Lord and God,
   and share more fully in his risen life. Amen.

PRAYER FOR THE EASTER SEASON

We behold your glory, O God,
    in the love shown by your Son,
lifted up on the cross
    and exalted on high.
Increase our love for one another,
    that both in name and in truth
we may be disciples of the risen Lord Jesus,
    and so reflect by our lives
        the glory that is yours. Amen.

PENTECOST PRAYER

God most high, origin and font
    of all renewal and love,
may the joy of the good news
    proclaimed by the apostles
resound in every language among all peoples,
    and within every culture.
May your Spirit bestow upon the whole world
    the regenerating power of your Son's resurrection.
In Christ's name, we pray. Amen.

FEAST OF PENTECOST

Come, Holy Spirit,
and from heaven direct on us the rays of your light.
— Come, God of the Poor;
— Come, Giver of Gifts;
— Come, Light of our Hearts.
Kindly Paraclete,
    shine on the hearts of your faithful,
  even into their darkest corners;
    for without your aid we falter.
Rain down your grace on the parched
  and heal the injured.
Give your Seven Holy Gifts to us, your faithful,
  for our trust is in you.
Enrich us with the gift of your peace.
Come Holy Spirit, fill the hearts of your faithful
  and kindle in us the fire of your love.
We ask this through Christ our Lord. Amen.

Key to photos

Acknowledgments

The Scripture quotations contained in the daily prayer section are from *New American Bible* (unless designated) copyright 1991, 1986, and 1970 by the Confraternity of Christian Doctrine, Washington, D.C. and used by permission of the copyright owner.

The Scripture quotations contained in the seasonal prayer section are from the *New Revised Standard Version Bible: Catholic Edition* copyright 1993 and 1989 by the Division of Christian Education of the National Council of the Churches of Christ in the U.S.A.

The text of the alternative opening prayers from *The Roman Missal* © 1973; the Scripture-related opening prayers and seasonal feast prayers from *The Sacramentary* (Revised Edition) © 1994; "Before Meals" and "After Meals" from *Book of Blessings* © 1989, International Committee on English in the Liturgy, Inc. (ICEL). All rights reserved.

"Blessing of Advent Wreath," "Blessing of the Tree," "Blessing of the Creche," "Blessing of the New Year" by David Philippart reprinted from *Welcome Yule* © 1995 Archdiocese of Chicago; Liturgy Training Publications, Chicago, Ill. Used with permission. All rights reserved.

"For Inner Healing," "Healing of a Relationship" by Nancy Benvenga from *Speaking to God* © 1993 courtesy of Ave Maria Press, Notre Dame, Ind. Used with permission. All rights reserved.

"An Indian Prayer," © 1989 courtesy of Red Cloud Indian School, Pine Ridge, South Dakota. Used with permission. Red Cloud Indian School is located on the Pine Ridge Indian Reservation in South Dakota. Please write regarding volunteer opportunities. Red Cloud Indian School, Pine Ridge, S. Dak.

"Prayer of One Who Feels Rejected," "Prayer for those Suffering with Illness" by Vienna Cobb Anderson from *Prayers of Our Hearts in Word and Action* © 1991 courtesy of Crossroads Publishing Company, New York, N.Y. Used with permission. All rights reserved.

"Morning Offering" by William O'Malley from *Daily Prayers for Busy People* © 1990 courtesy of St. Mary's Press, Winona, Minn. Used with permission. All rights reserved.

"The Road Ahead" by Thomas Merton from *Thoughts in Solitude* © 1958 courtesy of the Abbey of Our Lady of Gethsemani. Copyright renewed by the trustees of the Thomas Merton Legacy Trust. Reprinted by permission of Farrar, Straus and Giroux, Inc.

"Examination of Conscience for College Students" by Fr. George Matanic, O.P., was reprinted from the January 1996 *Crossroads Newsletter of the National Association of Campus Ministers*.

"Prayer for Easter," Creative Communications for the Parish, Inc. Used with permission.

"Prayer for the Poor," from *Being our Neighbor* © 1998. USCCB, Washington, D.C. Used with permission.

Prayer quote by Martin Helldorfer taken from *Prayer When it's Hard to Pray*, 23rd Publications. Used with permission.

An attempt was made to seek permission for all prepublished prayers contained in this prayer book. If, through inadvertence, anything has been printed without proper permission, acknowledgment will be made in future printings after notice has been received.

Special Thanks

To Rev. Peter Rocca, c.s.c., and Keara Coughlin, who served as advisors and editorial support, Paul Wieber and the Notre Dame Media Group for design and production, and Matt Cashore for principal photography.

I said to the man who stood at the gate of the year, "Give me a light that I may tread safely into the unknown." And he replied, "Go out into the darkness and put your hand into the hand of God. That shall be to you better than the light, and safer than a known way."

M.L. HASKINS